ANTIGUA AND BARBUDA

Sara Louise Kras

mc **Marshall Cavendish**
Benchmark
New York

ACKNOWLEDGMENTS
Thanks to Karen Knowles and Elizabeth Mason of the Antigua and Barbuda Tourism Board for arranging transportation, accommodations, and tour guides for me while I visited Antigua and Barbuda. Also, thanks to Galleon Beach Hotel at English Harbor, North Beach Lodge in Barbuda, and Long Bay Hotel in Antigua for providing me with places to stay.

PICTURE CREDITS
Cover photo: © Joe Kras
AFP: 93 • age fotostock/P.Narayan: 19 • age fotostock/World Pictures: 98 • AP: 37, 47 • Audrius Tomonis: 135 • Besstock: 63, 69, 72, 80, 94, 125, 126, 128, 129 • Claudio Bacinello: 106 • Corbis: 35, 39, 42 • Eye Ubiquitous/Kevin Nicol: 51 • Houserstock: 7 • Hutchison/Philip Wolmuth: 53 • International Photobank: 9, 56, 68, 79, 124 • Joe Kras: 3, 4, 5, 6, 8, 12, 14, 22, 24, 31, 33, 45, 48, 50, 52, 67, 76, 83, 90, 97, 100, 105, 108, 110, 127 • Michael Defreitas: 116, 117 • Photolibrary: 1, 10, 13, 15, 16, 17 (royalty free), 20, 25, 26, 27,28, 30, 40, 49, 55, 58, 59, 62, 65, 70, 75, 86, 87, 88, 89, 103, 104, 107, 109, 113, 114, 115, 118, 121, 123, 130 • Still Pictures: 60, 61 • Tropix.co.uk/Lynn Seldon: 64 • Tropix.co.uk/Maria Afonso: 23

PRECEDING PAGE
A group of Antiguan and Barbudan schoolboys.

Publisher (U.S.): Michelle Bisson
Editors: Christine Florie, Stephanie Pee, Sharon Low
Copyreader: Abby Collier
Designer: Lock Hong Liang
Cover picture researcher: Connie Gardner
Picture researchers: Thomas Khoo, Joshua Ang

Marshall Cavendish Benchmark
99 White Plains Road
Tarrytown, NY 10591
Web site: www.marshallcavendish.us

Originated and designed by Times Media Private Limited
An imprint of Marshall Cavendish International (Asia) Private Limited
A member of Times Publishing Limited

All Internet sites were correct and accurate at the time of printing. All monetary figures in this publication are in U.S. dollars.

Library of Congress Cataloging-in-Publication Data
Kras, Sara Louise.
  Antigua and Barbuda / by Sara Louise Kras.
    p. cm. — (Cultures of the world)
  Summary: "Provides comprehensive information on the geography, history, governmental structure, economy, cultural diversity, peoples, religion, and culture of Antigua and Barbuda"—Provided by publisher.
  Includes bibliographical references and index.
  ISBN-13: 978-0-7614-2570-0
  1. Antigua and Barbuda—Juvenile literature. I. Title. II. Series.

F2035.K73 2007
972.974—dc22   2006031537

Printed in China
7 6 5 4 3 2 1

CONTENTS

The ruins of Great George
Fort are located on
Monks Hill in southwest
Antigua.

Martello Towers on Barbuda are small, defensive forts built by the British in the 19th century.

INTRODUCTION

ANTIGUA AND BARBUDA IS A twin-island country surrounded by the Caribbean Sea. They are surrounded by coastlines with white-and-pink sandy beaches, reefs, and coves, with clear, blue water gently lapping their shores.

The majority of Antiguans and Barbudans are descendants of African slaves. These slaves were brought to the islands in the 17th century by the British to work on sugar plantations. Although the slaves were emancipated in 1834, the islands remained under the control of Great Britain for another one and a half centuries. After the inhabitants of the islands demanded independence from British rule, democratic elections began in 1980 with the country being led by Vere Cornwall Bird of the Antigua Labor Party. Antigua and Barbuda has since risen from slavery to independence after being under the yoke of slavery for over 150 years.

The sugar trade, the main source of income for Antigua and Barbuda in the past, has since been replaced by tourism. People come from all over the world to visit these pristine islands. Today, this democratic country is known for its safe ports, world-class sailing races, beautiful beaches, and offshore banking.

GEOGRAPHY

ANTIGUA AND BARBUDA IS LOCATED in a large group of islands called the West Indies. They are situated between the Atlantic Ocean and the Caribbean Sea and between North and South America. The two islands of Antigua and Barbuda are part of the northern portion of the West Indies called the Lesser Antilles.

The Lesser Antilles are made up of several islands. The main ones are Antigua, Barbuda, and Redonda. Some of the outer, smaller islands are Crump Island, Great Bird, and Guiana. Of these, Antigua and Barbuda are the only inhabited islands, with 98 percent of the population

Left: Yachts and boats dock at busy English Harbour. In the background lies Falmouth Harbour.

Opposite: **Barbuda's Two Foot Bay Beach is typical** of the kind of pristine beaches that can be found all over Antigua and Barbuda.

Large limestone cliffs loom over the Barbudan landscape.

living on Antigua and the other 2 percent residing on Barbuda. These islands are about 430 miles (692 km) north of Venezuela in South America. Antigua and Barbuda cover a total land area of 171 square miles (443 square km), about 2.5 times the size of Washington, DC.

Antigua had a volcanic beginning but today has no active volcanoes. With the passage of time, three distinct land types developed on the island of Antigua: the southwestern volcanic region, the rolling plains in the central section, and the uplands located in the northeastern area. Volcanic sediment can be found to the west, and limestone plates appear on the east side of the island, almost dividing it in two. Along its white sand coast are many inlets and bays. A large protected harbor called English Harbour is located on the south shore.

The land mass of Barbuda is slightly different in that it is made of ancient coral reefs, limestone, and low-rising sand dunes. On the western side of the island is Codrington Lagoon, which opens up into the sea. The central area of the island is flat, whereas the eastern region has high tablelands with limestone cliffs and caves.

BEACHES, BEACHES, AND MORE BEACHES

Antigua is known for having 365 beaches, one for every day of the year. Its coastline is scattered with numerous bays and coves lined with reefs, along with white sand beaches lapped by crystal blue water.

Galley Bay is along the northwest coast of the Caribbean side of the island. It is known for its crashing waves. Next to it is Hawksbill Bay, named after Hawksbill Rock, which is located offshore. The rock resembles the head of a Hawksbill turtle, from which its name was originally derived.

The southwest and south coast is scattered with hills. At 1,330 feet (405 m), the island's highest elevation point, Boggy Peak, is located

The beaches in Antigua and Barbuda lure tourists to the islands.

on the southwestern corner of Antigua. On the south shore is English Harbor. Yachts and boats are often docked in this protected area. Some of the beaches in this area can only be reached by vehicles with four-wheel drive.

Located in the hills of the south coast is green limestone, which is quarried and used for building churches, houses, and roads.

A national park called Half Moon Bay is on the east coast of Antigua. This bay has a beautiful beach. On the easternmost side of the island is Long Bay, where the water is a clear turquoise blue, and the protected reef is filled with a wide variety of colorful fish.

Also in this area is a limestone arch called Devil's Bridge. Milky-white waves carved out this beautiful natural phenomenon over a period of time and now crash through its blowholes and against its volcanic rock. Deep narrow crevasses line the stony surface from which growling sounds echo, emitted by the treacherous waters below. The arch received the name Devil's Bridge during the time of slavery because so many black slaves jumped off it to commit suicide. It was thought that the devil was in the area.

Barbuda is a low-lying coral island about 27 miles (43.5 km) north of Antigua with its highest point only 125 feet (38.1 m) above sea level. It has miles and miles of pristine beaches made of white-and-pink sand. The pink sand is made of crushed conch shells.

CLIMATE

The weather in Antigua and Barbuda is warm and sunny all year long. Even though there is some seasonal change, the average temperature is 81°F (27°C). Because the islands have a tropical climate, temperatures can rise as high as 93°F (33°C) between May and October. However, sea breezes called trade winds help to cool the air.

The annual rainfall is about 40 inches (100 cm). The months of August and September usually the receive the most rain.

Antigua lies within the hurricane belt, which consists of areas vulnerable to hurricanes. As a result, it has been affected by a number

TRADE WINDS

The reason why Antigua is such a popular sailing destination is because of the existence of trade winds. These are winds that continuously blow toward the equator. Christopher Columbus is accredited with discovering them. He used these winds to cross the Atlantic Ocean. Sailors on trade ships named these winds "trade winds" because they helped facilitate trade.

UNUSUAL TREES

Two trees in Antigua and Barbuda have a strange history. The Sandbox tree (*below*) has thick spikes along its trunk. In the past it was known as the agony tree, as slaves were tied to its spiky trunk while they were being whipped. Its sap is also very harmful, causing blindness if it comes in contact with your eyes.

Silk cotton trees in Antigua were not chopped down in the past because an ancient African voodoo belief suggested that spirits inhabited them. This tree is also very useful because it produces a fruit which contains seeds surrounded by cottony fibers. During World War II these fibers were used in life vests to help with flotation in water.

of hurricanes. Hurricane season lasts from July to November. In September 1995 Antigua and Barbuda were hit hard by Hurricane Luis. By the time the storm subsided, thousands of houses had been damaged or completely destroyed. In 1999 Hurricane Jose whipped the islands with 100 mph (160 kph) winds and torrential rains. Power lines were cut, trees were ripped out by the roots, and roofs of houses were blown off.

The government of Antigua and Barbuda had issued an early warning to its citizens about Hurricane Jose. The Red Cross, in collaboration with the National Disaster Office, began preparing volunteers and staff for the upcoming storm. Stockpiles of blankets and tarps were stored, and citizens were evacuated from high-risk areas. This support system helped cut back on instances of death and injury during the hurricane.

The fruit of the breadfruit tree has many uses.

FLORA

It is hard to establish the original indigenous plants of Antigua and Barbuda because of the intense colonization during the sugarcane era that stripped the islands of their natural forests. Furthermore, over the years, varieties of plants were introduced into the country's ecology by settlers from different parts of the world. Some of the plants were from neighboring Central and South America, but others came from as far away as Asia and Africa.

Coconut trees, Cretan date palms, calabash, and breadfruit grow on Antigua and Barbuda. The versatile fruit from this tree can be baked, roasted, or made into a casserole. Another useful tree is the tamarind. Its seeds are boiled and dried. They are then used by local women

The Agave lily has an unusual foliage.

to make placemats, coasters, bracelets, necklaces, and bags that are sold to visiting tourists.

The national tree is the whitewood tree. It is related to almond and mangrove trees. It grows mainly next to dry river beds and in the coastal areas of Antigua. Its wood is very hard and strong and resists decay because it does not rot very easily even in the humid tropics. In the past, flooring, gates, carts, and benches were made from the whitewood tree. Because of its usefulness, many were chopped down and today there are very few of these trees left.

Located on the southern part of Antigua is Fig Tree Drive. Fig means banana in Antigua and the road is lined with the trees. There are different types of bananas that grow here, such as the lady finger banana, which is smaller than a banana and can be eaten in a variety of ways. However, the plantain, another variety of banana, should only be eaten fried or boiled.

A variety of herbal and flowering plants can be found throughout Antigua and Barbuda, such as the seaside grape, black willow, bougainvillea, hibiscus, oleander, candelabra cactus, and barrel cactus. Antigua also has ponds scattered throughout the island that are filled with lotus blossoms.

The national flower of Antigua and Barbuda is the Agave. It is part of the lily family. Its name comes from the Greek *agave* meaning "noble." The Agave grows in dry areas, such as the woodland hills. It stores water in the fleshy leaves at its base. Growing from the base are tall flower

stalks up to 20 feet (6 m) high. Its golden flowers bloom only once every 10 to 20 years, then die. Another name for this plant is the century plant because it blooms so infrequently.

FAUNA

There are three distinct types of animals that live in Antigua and Barbuda: animals in the air, on land, and in the water.

In the air, one can find fruit bats and free-tailed bats. Free-tailed bats are the most common. Using echolocation, they find insects and feast on them. Other flying animals are the pelican, cattle egret (locally called *gauling*), osprey, hummingbird, red-billed tropicbird (locally called *chichichawa*), and the West Indian Whistling-Duck, known for its sharp whistling sound.

On the ground one can find mongooses, donkeys, and goats. The mongoose was brought to Jamaica from India in 1872 to kill rats and snakes on sugarcane plantations. Eventually, it was brought to

Antigua and Barbuda is the only eastern Caribbean country where the European fallow deer can be found.

Antigua. Mongooses are seen all over the island of Antigua walking warily across a road or yard. However, there are no mongooses in Barbuda, and if someone is caught bringing one to the island, that person is imprisoned.

The European fallow deer is the national animal of Antigua. In all the eastern Caribbean countries, deer can only be found on Antigua and Barbuda. This is why it was named the national animal. This deer is not indigenous to Antigua and Barbuda. Instead, its roots are thought to be from England. It was brought to the islands by the Codrington family, a well-known family in Antigua and Barbuda history.

In 1784 there were up to 3,000 head of deer living on Barbuda, but by 1827 they were considered a pest because they stripped the land of local vegetation. When Bethell Codrington bought Guiana Island, a small island 300 feet (91 m) from the island of Antigua, deer were taken there to be raised as stock or meat. Currently, this national animal can be found living happily on the Barbuda and Guiana islands in small numbers.

There are several reptiles living on Antigua and Barbuda, such as the land turtle, gecko, tree lizard, racer snake, toad, and tree frog. The land turtle was introduced to Antigua by Native American Indians and European settlers. Sailors stored land turtles on their canoes or ships as a constant source of fresh meat on long sea voyages. Today, these turtles are sometimes kept as pets.

A variety of insects live on the islands, such as the cicada, horse spider, firefly, and honeybee. The honeybee is not native to Antigua.

It was brought over from Europe during the 18th century to provide honey for the islanders. Butterflies are also common. It is not unusual to see hundreds of them flitting through the air.

In the surrounding sea live humpback whales, green turtles, barracuda, albacore, groupers, yellow-tailed snappers, flying fish, and dolphins, which can sometimes be seen hunting stingrays that leap out of the water as they try to escape. Corals and shellfish also make the seawaters their home. In addition, there are lobsters, smooth brain corals, white sea urchins, land crabs, Caribbean oysters, queen conchs, and southern stingrays that glide through the water like elegant birds. These stingrays measure 6 feet (1 m) from wing tip to wing tip.

Stingrays with their formidable wingspan can be found in the surrounding waters of Antigua and Barbuda.

In some areas of Barbuda the beaches are littered with empty queen conch shells. The conch can grow up to 10 inches long. This mollusk has a rubbery meat that is a favorite West Indian food. Its shell is lined with a pretty pink and peach color and is often used to decorate yards or houses.

ANTIGUAN AND BARBUDAN TOWNS

Scattered throughout the island of Antigua are small villages. But the majority of people on the island live in the capital city of Saint John's. Barbuda has only one village, Codrington, where the majority of its inhabitants reside.

THE HISTORY OF REDONDA

Redonda is the remains of a volcanic cone and is the smallest island in the Lesser Antilles. It is located 35 miles (56 km) southwest of Antigua. It reaches 984 feet (300 m) high and spans 0.77 miles (1.25 km) long. Because of the large amount of seabird droppings, Redonda was mined for bird guano in the 1860s, which was used in fertilizers. Later, aluminum phosphate, a valuable component of gunpowder, was discovered under the guano, so mining operations were established. At one point, about 100 miners worked on Redonda. A cableway using baskets was built to transfer the mined phosphate to a pier for shipping.

After World War I, a small mining crew remained on the rocky island to maintain the equipment. This continued until 1929 when a hurricane destroyed most of the mining buildings. No one lives on the island today.

Saint John's is a sheltered cove located on the northwest side of Antigua. Its main port, Deepwater Harbor, is also located there. It is home to about 28,000 people. This historical town dates back to the 17th century, when it became the administrative center for Antigua and Barbuda. Today, it is the capital of the country and the seat of government. Because of the many cruise ships that visit this port, its harbor has been dredged to allow the megaships to dock.

Saint John's still maintains its old-world charm. One of its oldest buildings is the courthouse, which was constructed around 1750.

Low-rise buildings line the streets of Saint John's, the capital of Antigua and Barbuda.

Originally, the courthouse was used by the Supreme Court and the Houses of Parliament. Today, it is used as the Museum of Antigua and Barbuda. Another historical building is Saint John's Cathedral. Its baroque towers dominate the skyline.

Throughout the city there are still several 18th- and 19th-century buildings. Some were town houses for plantation owners. Other historical reminders are the metal boot cleaners located next to the sidewalks. They were used hundreds of years ago to scrape mud off boots. During the sugarcane era, the sidewalks were built like stairs with high and low steps. The low steps were for the men, and the high ones were for the women to help them get into a carriage.

The historic Redcliffe Quay was originally used as a holding area for cargo during the 18th century. Goods such as cotton, sugar, sheepskins, and tobacco were held there. This quay also contained a slave-holding compound. Thames Street, beginning at Redcliffe Quay, was where the slaves were lined up and inspected by future buyers. This event was called the parade. People would come from all the other islands to attend the parade and purchase new slaves. Today, tourists flock to Redcliffe Quay to purchase clothing, jewelry, toys, and other items.

Just a couple of miles outside Saint John's is Fort James. This historical fort contains 10 cannons. Each cannon weighs 2.5 tons (2,449 kg) and required 11 men to fire just one shot. Each shot could travel a distance of 1.5 miles (2.41 km). Even so, Fort James was never utilized in battle.

CODRINGTON This village of 1,400 is home to the majority of people who live on Barbuda. It was settled as the main residential center of the island in the 17th century. King Charles II granted a 50-year lease to Christopher and John Codrington, powerful landholders, on June 5, 1685. The Codringtons used the island to make and prepare supplies that were shipped to their plantations in Antigua and other eastern Caribbean islands. The slaves had their own small homes in Codrington.

Today, Codrington is a quiet village. Many of its buildings and stone walls are from the 17th and 18th century. In addition, some wells, hundreds of years old, are still used today to supply Barbudans with their water.

Located in the center of Codrington Village is the Government House, which dates back to 1694. The Holy Trinity School uses the stables of this building as classrooms for a primary school. The main house was damaged by Hurricane Luis in 1995 and still has not been repaired.

The government body of Barbuda, the Barbuda Council, uses one of the buildings in the ginnery. This building served as a storage area for salt and cotton during the slave era.

Opposite: **A family strolls along the sleepy streets of Codrington on the island of Barbuda.**

21

HISTORY

PEOPLE HAVE INHABITED ANTIGUA since around 2900 B.C. Evidence of early settlements was found near current-day Parhram. Another ancient site which dates back to 1775 B.C. was also found in the Jolly Beach area.

On Barbuda a Stone Age site that dates back to 1875 B.C. near Martello Tower was found. Ancient Amerindians lived in Antigua and Barbuda until about 100 B.C.

The Ceramic Age slowly started around 775 B.C. when Amerindians from mainland South America, called Arawaks, began to arrive in dugout canoes. They made pottery and were farmers. They planted a variety of crops, such as pineapples, cotton, and peanuts. But their main food staple was the cassava root, which was planted in abundance.

After A.D. 1200 a new group of Amerindians arrived, the Caribs. Even though they were warlike, they began mixing with the existing Arawaks. Through this combination a new group called Island Caribs was formed. These were the people existing in Antigua and Barbuda when Europeans arrived in the 16th century.

In 1493 Christopher Columbus sighted Antigua. He named it after the miracle-working saint of Seville, Santa Maria la Antigua. The Island Caribs already had a name for Antigua, which was Wadadli, today the name of Antiguan beer.

There is no evidence that Columbus saw Barbuda. After Columbus, both the Spanish and the French attempted to settle there without success because of raiding Arawak Indians.

The first permanent European residents of Antigua were the English, who came from the Caribbean island of St. Kitts in 1632. Once they arrived

Above: **A statue of Christopher Columbus who first sighted Antigua in the 16th century.**

Opposite: **Weights and measurements used in colonial Antigua.**

A fort at Shirley Heights was originallly built to protect the British sugar trade.

they claimed Antigua for the English Crown. This group of people were under the leadership of Sir Thomas Warner, who was instrumental in colonizing many of the Leeward Islands. They established a small settlement with numerous farms. They were attacked at various times by the Island Caribs, as well as the French and Dutch. But the English persisted and became permanent residents. The threat of Island Carib attacks eventually dissipated, as there is no further historical reference to the Island Caribs on Antigua after 1705.

In the early 1600s, tobacco was the main crop produced on the Leeward Islands. Because tobacco was harmful to the soil, its production was stopped in the mid-1600s. Sugarcane was soon grown in bountiful abundance.

The demand for sugar grew, creating a continuous triangle of trade. Goods such as guns, textiles, and horses were brought from Europe to Africa. These goods were exchanged with the local tribes living along the coasts of Africa for black slaves. The slaves were then sailed to the Caribbean and sold to sugarcane plantation owners at a high price. Payment was usually made in sugar, rum, or molasses (a thick brown sugar syrup); this new cargo was then shipped to Europe and sold at a high profit before the cycle started over all again. The sugar industry was extremely important to the economics of England. Therefore, England needed to protect its interest in the sugar trade against the French and the Spanish. To accomplish this the British Navy established English Harbor in Antigua and many other forts around the island.

THE SUGARCANE ERA

In 1674 Sir Christopher Codrington arrived from Barbados, where he was a powerful landowner, and established a large sugar plantation on Antigua. He brought in slaves from Africa to work on his plantation. He also brought the latest techniques for growing sugarcane and used windmill technology. Because Antigua's land was flat with strong trade winds, it was a prime location for windmills that drove the sugarcane crushers. These huge crushers were originally built out of Lignum vitae wood, which was indigenous to Antigua and incredibly strong.

A painting depicting a typical scene of slaves harvesting sugarcane during the era of colonial British rule.

HOW SUGARCANE WAS MADE INTO SUGAR

Once the freshly chopped sugarcane arrived at the mill, it was fed into three heavy rollers and was crushed (*right*). Slaves were very careful not to get too close to the rollers for fear of a hand or even an arm being completely smashed. The huge sails of the mill moved the crushing rollers about four times a minute. The command "Turn her out!" was used to start the mill and "Turn her in!" to stop it.

While the cane passed through the rollers, a green sugar juice would start to drip into a pan below. The pan dumped into a wooden gutter that led to the boiling house. The leftover crushed stalks were spread out and dried in the sun and were later used to keep the fires going in the boiling house.

Slaves who worked in the hot boiling house removed the impurities in the sugar by adding lime to the sugar juice. The juice was then placed in huge, open cast-iron or copper tanks. The sugar juice was heated until the water evaporated and until it became thick like caramel and turned a brown color.

The sugar was then spooned into large wooded boxes to crystallize. Once it was crystallized it was taken out of the boxes and placed in wooden barrels or clay pots and put in the curing house to dry for about two to three weeks. After the curing was complete, the sugar was sealed and shipped to Europe to be sold in the markets.

Because of Codrington's financial success, more windmills followed. By 1748 there were some 175 windmills dotting the countryside of Antigua. The remains of some of them can still be found today.

In addition to their sugar plantations, Christopher Codrington and his brother John were given permission by the British monarch to lease the island of Barbuda. The lease was for a set period of time. The rent payment was established as one fat sheep yearly. Christopher Codrington also served as the governor of Antigua from September 1689 to July 1698.

The Codringtons were allowed to renew their lease of Barbuda by Queen Anne in 1705 for 99 years. Barbuda was sometimes used as a vacation spot for the Codringtons and their wealthy friends. The island was stocked with deer and boar, so the Codringtons could take their friends on hunting trips. Several hunting lodges were constructed and their ruins can still be found all over the island today.

African and white slaves were housed on the island, as well as livestock such as sheep, cattle, hogs, and hens. The slaves on Barbuda were much freer than the Antiguan slaves because there were no sugarcane fields to work in. Punishment for rebellious slaves on Barbuda was to be sent to Antigua to work the fields.

Even though Barbuda was not used to grow sugarcane, it was still a very profitable island for the Codringtons. The Atlantic side of the island was surrounded by a shallow reef where passing ships sometimes met their demise. The cargo and equipment from shipwrecks earned Codrington a good sum of money, as he could sell it once it was salvaged. To expedite the process and also increase profits, slaves were instructed to place large torches near the reef. Captains of passing ships thought the torches were fires on land. They would steer their vessels toward the fire and crash into the reef. Slaves would swim out to the sunken ship and loot its treasures. Ruins of a

On Barbuda, ruins are all that remain of a storehouse used to keep the treasures of shipwrecked vessels.

storage house for salvaged goods can still be found near Two Foot Bay on the northeastern side of the island. Today, 145 shipwrecks have been documented off the coast of Barbuda.

NELSON'S DOCKYARD

Nelson's Dockyard was named in honor of Admiral Horatio Nelson.

Because of the valuable cargo being shipped to and from the Caribbean, it became the site of a power struggle between Britain, France, Spain, and Portugal. Britain employed the use of its powerful navy to protect its interests in the eastern Caribbean. One of its main naval bases was

established in English Harbor, Antigua. It began as a naval dockyard in 1725 when funds were set aside for its construction. The facilities built created a safe haven for British ships in the Caribbean. The harbor protected the ships from marauding pirates or devastating hurricanes. It also served as a ship-repair station: a place where ships could have broken masts rebuilt, sails repaired, and barnacles scraped off their hulls. Repairing royal naval warships was the most important function at the harbor. These ships were used to protect British colonies and capture other sugar islands of the French, Spanish, or Portuguese, which in turn increased the wealth of Britain.

CAREENING THE SHIPS

Careen means "to lay a ship on its side for repairs," which includes fixing leaks or scraping barnacles off the hull. Nelson's Dockyard was set up to careen large ships. Capstans, cylinders that cables were wound around, were built in Nelson's Dockyard to assist in this process. Several capstan bars or poles were used as levers to wind the cables. All of this was done with manpower. In Nelson's Dockyard, a man was placed between each slot of the capstan bars while a fiddler stood on top of the cylinder. When the winding process started, the fiddler began to play to encourage the men during this hard work.

Careening a ship required the following steps:

1. Tying a ship to a wharf that was near deep water.
2. Removing all heavy and loose objects on board.
3. Removing the topmasts.
4. Attaching a framework with rope that was connected to a capstan.
5. Slowly tilting the ship on its side by winding the capstan.
6. Repairing one side of the ship's bottom.
7. Repeating the process for the other side of the ship.

The structures in the dockyard were made of local stone and brick from Europe. The brick was used as ballast in the bottom of incoming ships and was off-loaded at the dockyard to be used as building material. To hold the stones together, the British used sand from the beaches and made mortar. This harbor was known as the best British harbor in the West Indies.

The majority of buildings seen today on the harbor were built between 1785 and 1792. During some of this time (1784–87), Admiral Horatio Nelson was stationed there. The dockyard was named in his honor and today is known as Nelson's Dockyard.

Formerly the copper and lumber store, it has since been converted into a hotel at English Harbour.

NATIONAL HISTORIC SYMBOL

Sugar mill towers represent Antigua's history, when men and women were oppressed in slavery. To create a national historical symbol, the mills at Betty's Hope (*below*) were selected for restoration. Betty's Hope's history is very much a part of Antigua's history. The sugar plantation was established by Christopher Keynall in about 1650.

Betty's Hope was later awarded to Christopher Codrington by the British crown in 1674. Slaves by the hundreds were shipped to Antigua. By 1720 the population on Antigua was made up of about 84 percent African slaves. A slave inventory was made in 1751 at Betty's Hope. In total there were 277 slaves; in part these slaves consisted of 39 men and 59 women who worked in the fields, 20 boys and 26 girls who did light work, and 49 who were either too old or too young to work. The number of slaves increased, and by 1780 there were a total of 393 slaves on the plantation.

The Codringtons sold Betty's Hope to the Antigua Sugar Estates Ltd. in 1944. By 1990 the Betty's Hope Trust was formed and renovations began on the sugar mill tower. Rebuilding a sugar mill was no easy task, as modern day workers had no idea how they were built in days long ago. Much research had to be done before the restoration could proceed. Today, visitors can go to these mills to see how a working sugar mill tower operates.

Many rules were established to keep peace and order on the dockyard. Women were not allowed on the dockyard because they caused distractions, and smoking was not allowed because of the large amounts of gunpowder in the area.

Fort Berkeley, located on a strip of land at the entrance of the harbor, was established to protect the dockyard. Because of these strong fortifications, Antigua was never overtaken by another European power.

In 1961 Nelson's Dockyard was named a historical monument of Antigua and in 1985 was established as a national park. Today, it is part of a large national park that includes the Dockyard Museum and the old Admiral's House. In the museum, visitors can view various 18th-century artifacts of battles at sea and raiding pirates. Other buildings that have been restored in the dockyard are the pitch and tar store, the old guard house, the copper and lumber store, and the officer's quarters.

WATTLE HOUSES

Even though most Antiguan laborers were finally realizing they had workers' rights, extreme poverty still existed. Many people lived in wattle houses, which were built and lived in until the 1940s. These houses were made of woven sticks that were plastered together with mud, also known as wattle and daub. The roof was made from the waste products of the sugarcane plants. The one-room homes often had bare dirt floors. It was not uncommon for families with six to eight members to live in one home.

Sanitation was nonexistent. It was common for bugs called jiggers to inhabit the dirt floor, giving the occupants of the house nasty bites. Clothing for these poor laborers were made from burlap sacks or old flour bags.

In 1951 two hurricanes destroyed the majority of wattle houses in Antigua. Once these flimsy, uncomfortable homes were blown down, no one bothered to rebuild them.

ANTIGUA'S VOLCANIC NEIGHBOR

Even though Antigua and Barbuda had political problems, it was hospitable to its neighbor Montserrat. In 1996 and 1997 a volcano erupted on this nearby island country, completely covering its capital city in ash, huge rocks, and other debris. The hospital, airport, Catholic church, and hundreds of residents' homes were totally buried.

Even though the city had been completely evacuated a year before its eruption, no one knew for sure when the volcano would explode, so some people began moving back into the capital city prior to the eruption and 19 people were ultimately killed. After the huge explosion, refugees poured out of Montserrat. To help these refugees the Antiguan government allowed 3,000 to settle in Antigua, swelling its population.

During the explosion some of the ash blew over into Antigua, covering cars and houses with a thick layer of dust. People wore masks to protect their lungs. Small earthquakes shook the streets in Saint John's and outer villages.

Since then the volcano has had other large explosions, one in 2002 and another in 2003, when one of the lava domes collapsed, sending ash up to about 50,000 feet. On a clear night Antiguans can still see the glowing lava dome on their neighboring island.

PIRATES SAILING THE CARIBBEAN

Up to the 18th century, Antigua and Barbuda was still in danger of being attacked by pirates. There are many stories of such attacks. One such story is about a pirate named Captain Daniel in the late 17th century. He and his men stormed the island of Barbuda and attacked the Codrington manor. The pirates burned down houses and took 15 slaves.

The British government received several pleas from its colonies for protection against raiding pirates. Ships attempting to reach Antigua's shores with goods for sale and trade were often attacked by these bandits. One such bandit was the pirate Captain Finn. There was much celebration in Antigua when he and five of his men were hanged in 1723. Afterward, their dead bodies were displayed as a warning along the water's edge to other pirates.

Antiguan plantation owners and the British government funded the building of several forts to protect the island. One was called Shirley Heights and was built overlooking the Caribbean Sea. Included in the complex were artillery quarters, officer quarters, a large fort, a cemetery, and a hospital. It was used as a lookout for incoming ships. If a ship was spotted, a flag was raised in the air. Through a series of flag systems around the island, Saint John's and the entire island could be alerted within 15 minutes of an incoming ship and whether it was an enemy or friend.

EMANCIPATION OF ANTIGUAN AND BARBUDAN SLAVES

Throughout the era of slavery, there were several slave uprisings on the two islands. Finally in 1834 slavery came to an end in Antigua and

Barbuda. This was one year after Great Britain passed an act eradicating slavery throughout its empire. Liberta was the first free village in Antigua and Barbuda, followed by Freetown and Freeman's Village.

Even though the slaves had been freed, they still had to earn money to survive, and many had to continue working for their plantation owners. They lived in the same ramshackle huts as before and were forced to work as laborers for inferior pay with very little rights. A worker could be sent to jail and whipped for the smallest offense. In addition, murders of black workers occurred with very little investigation by the local government to find who was responsible.

Riots broke out a few times with the offenders shot on the spot by police. Black workers rarely questioned or demanded better treatment from the plantation owners, because if they did, it was highly likely that they or their family would be killed. Nevertheless, conflicts between workers and sugar plantation owners continued throughout the 19th and early 20th century. Between 1938 and 1939, Sir Walter Citrine, general secretary of the British Trades Union Congress, who was visiting the West Indies, founded the Antigua Trades and Labor Union.

BECOMING AN INDEPENDENT COUNTRY

In 1943 Vere Cornwall Bird was elected as the president of the Antigua Trades and Labor Union. This energetic leader fought long and hard for laborers' rights. The labor union eventually became the first political party formed for almost 30 years. It was later called the Antigua Labor Party (ALP).

In order to gain independence, Antigua joined the West Indies Federation in January 1958. But the federation was short-lived and it was disbanded in 1962. Antigua gained associated status with Great Britain in February 1967. With this status Antigua was responsible for its internal affairs and government, whereas Great Britain kept the responsibilities of managing Antigua's defense and foreign affairs. During the 1960s the sugar industry began to fail and by 1971 was completely shut down. In its place Antigua looked toward the tourism industry as a source of income.

Antigua still sought complete independence from Great Britain. Elections took place in April 1980, and the ALP won. On November 1, 1981, Antigua and Barbuda received their independence, jointly. Vere Cornwall Bird was named the first prime minister of Antigua. Barbuda sent a request to Great Britain to be its own nation, but its request was denied. As a result, the Barbuda's People Movement was formed, which continued to demand secession from Antigua.

Other political parties were formed in this new democracy, such as the United People's Movement, the Barbuda National Party, and the United National Democratic Party. Even so, throughout the 1980s the ALP, led by the Bird family, was the dominant force in politics.

In the past there have been accusations of corruption and criminal activity taking place in the government. These came to a head in April 1990, when the government of Antigua and Barbuda received an official letter of protest from the government of Colombia. The letter complained of illegal sales of firearms that were being supplied from Antigua to the drug traffickers in Colombia. A judicial inquiry took place, and Vere Bird Jr. was found guilty and banned from politics for life.

Later in 1999 the U.S. government issued a report that stated Antiguan banking laws were allowing money laundering, or disguising money

Antigua and Barbudan president, Vere Cornwall Bird (*right*) with president of Saint Kitts Labour Union, Robert Llewellyn Bradshaw (*left*).

from criminal activities. After this report great efforts were made by the Antiguan government to clean up these allegations and problems.

Intrigue and corruption continued to plague the government, which included the ALP and the prime minister. In 2001 there were fraud allegations against the minister of health and his conduct as head of the state-run Medical Benefits Scheme. He resigned, but an independent inquiry took place. The inquiry recommended that the Medical Benefits Scheme become an independent group, separate from the government. It also recommended that a prosecutor be appointed to look at charges brought against 12 people involved in the fraud. The prime minister,

Lester B. Bird was Antigua and Barbuda's prime minister for ten years after his father, Vere Bird, stepped down from office in 1994.

Lester Bird, was never directly implicated, but rumors circulated about his possible involvement.

In April 2002 Lester Bird had a public dispute with the leaders of the popular Progressive Party (UPP). He initiated a libel suit against these men that included the future prime minister, Baldwin Spencer. Lester Bird later dropped the suit.

Allegations of illegal activity mounted in May 2002 when an ALP member of Parliament, from Bird's own party, demanded Lester Bird's resignation, as well as that of his chief of staff. The UPP organized thousands of demonstrators in the streets demanding the same thing. It was not until March 2004 when the Bird family's power was finally usurped in the general elections.

Venezuelan President Hugo Chavez (right) welcomes Antigua and Barbuda prime minister Baldwin Spencer who succeeded Lester Bird as the new leader of Antigua and Barbuda in 2004.

GOVERNMENT

ANTIGUA AND BARBUDA ACHIEVED complete independence on November 1, 1981. Antigua and Barbuda were no longer under British colonial rule. Even so, they remained a constitutional monarchy, with the governor general appointed as head of state and considered a representative of the reigning British monarch. Antigua's British-style parliamentary system has three branches: executive, legislative, and judicial.

THE EXECUTIVE BRANCH

Members of the cabinet are selected from the legislative branch and appointed by the prime minister. The cabinet comprises the heads of different ministries such as: attorney general and minister of legal affairs, minister of finance and economy, minister of tourism and civil aviation, minister of education, minister of health, sports, and youth affairs, and minister of justice.

THE LEGISLATIVE BRANCH

This branch is bicameral, that is, it is made up of two legislative chambers. It consists of a 17-member House of Representatives that is elected by popular vote in elections that are held every five years. The Senate also has 17 members, but they are appointed by the leaders in government.

The purpose of the House of Representatives is to present new legislation. The Senate then reviews and approves any proposed legislation.

The leader of the party that holds the most seats in the House of Representatives becomes the prime minister. To ensure that the opposition is given a voice in government, the governor general appoints an opposition leader. The leader is typically one who receives the most support from members of the legislative branch who oppose the majority government.

Opposite: **Presidential campaign posters erected during the elections. The 2004 election in Antigua and Barbuda was one of the most hotly contested the country had ever seen.**

When appointed commissions are assembled, the leader of the opposition is included along with the governor general and the prime minister.

One of the duties of the prime minister includes appointing 11 of the 17 seats in the Senate with the approval of the governor general. One of these members must reside in Barbuda. The opposition leader must advise appointments for four senators to the governor general. One of the two remaining senators is appointed by the governor general and the other on the advice of the Barbuda Council.

THE JUDICIAL BRANCH

The magistrates of the judicial branch are appointed by the Office of the Attorney General in the executive branch. Even so, this branch remains comparatively independent of the legislative and executive branches.

The judicial branch is composed of the Magistrate's Court, which handles minor offenses, and the High Court, which deals with major offenses. The Magistrate's Courts are the main courts for Antigua and

THE NATIONAL FLAG OF ANTIGUA

The national flag was designed by art teacher Reginald Samuel in 1966. The sun represents the beginning of a new era for Antigua. The black background stands for African heritage and the soil. Red stands for the blood of enslaved ancestors and the energy of the people. Blue signifies the hope of the people. The large V shape embodies victory. The colors yellow, blue, and white stand for the sun, sea, and sand.

Barbuda. They are divided into three districts. Each district has a magistrate who is also a justice of the peace. This magistrate is responsible for conducting preliminary inquiries regarding criminal charges and for settling small civil claims.

To go beyond these local courts, a case can be passed to the Eastern Caribbean States Supreme Court located in Saint Lucia. This court consists of the Court of Appeal and a High Court of Justice. It acts as the superior court of record for Antigua and Barbuda, British Virgin Islands, Dominica, Grenada, Montserrat, Saint Kitts and Nevis, Anguilla, Saint Lucia, and Saint Vincent and the Grenadines. All are members of the Organization of Eastern Caribbean States (OECS).

The last court of appeal is located in London and is called the Judicial Committee of Privy Council. Once a decision is made by this court for any OECS member, it is final and cannot be appealed to any other court.

ELECTIONS

Rumors of rigged elections circulated during the rule of the Antigua Labor Party (ALP). Unethical tactics were thought to be used, such as disconnecting power to voter's homes, then agreeing to reconnect their electricity only if they promised to vote for the ALP. The party was also accused of burning down newspaper offices that printed bad press on the ALP. There were even rumors of voters who were given large sums of cash to vote for the ALP.

Because of public dissatisfaction with the ALP, the general election that took place on March 23, 2004, had a huge voter turnout. Ninety-one percent of all qualified voters came to the polls. Once the results were in, the

United Progressive Party (UPP) had won 12 of the 17 parliamentary seats. The leader of the UPP was Baldwin Spencer, who became the new prime minister on March 24, 2004.

THE BARBUDA COUNCIL

This council was established in 1976 and is responsible for running the internal affairs of the island of Barbuda. It consists of 11 members. Nine of these members are elected by voters of Barbuda. The other two are the Barbuda representative and senator of the legislative branch in the national government.

The purpose of the Barbuda Council is to control and oversee public health, public utilities, agriculture, forestry, and monitor road maintenance. It also raises and collects revenue to cover its expenses.

Laws are also passed by the council. One law forbids swearing in public. If the offender continues to break this law, he or she is thrown in jail and fined.

THE NATIONAL COAT OF ARMS

The coat of arms is topped with a pineapple, which represents the national fruit, the Antiguan black pineapple. On either side of the pineapple are hibiscus flowers, which represent the versatile plant life. The shield has a yellow sun above wavy blue and white bands. These symbolize the sun, sea, and sand of Antigua and Barbuda. The sugar mill in the center of the shield and the sugarcane stalk on the left are symbols of its sugarcane history. The century plant on the right is the national flower. The deer supporting the shield on either side stand for the animal life found on Antigua. The motto below the shield is printed in red on a yellow ribbon, stating: EACH ENDEAVOURING, ALL ACHIEVING.

Because Barbudans have such a dissimilar slave history to Antiguans, many of their laws are different. For example, those born in Barbuda or with Barbudan ancestry can claim any land on the island as their own. All they have to do is put up a fence to claim it. Even though this is part of Barbudan law, very few people live outside of Codrington.

The Barbudan Council government building is the meeting place for the Barbuda Council where matters pertaining to Barbuda internal matters are discussed.

THE CONSTITUTION

The Constitution of Antigua and Barbuda was established on October 31, 1981. This document defines the country and its goals. The section called "Protection of Fundamental Rights and Freedoms of the Individual" covers subjects such as protection from slavery and forced labor, meaning no person shall be held in slavery or servitude and no person shall be required to perform forced labor. Also covered is protection from inhumane treatment, meaning no person shall be subjected to torture or to inhumane or degrading punishment or other such treatment.

The constitution also establishes the different branches of the government and their purposes. It defines the regulations and restrictions of parliament. The police service commission rules are laid out. In addition, the constitution states what classifies citizenship.

NATIONAL ANTHEM

A competition was held in 1966 to establish a national anthem for Antigua. The musical composition by Walter Chambers, a church organist, was chosen. The accompanying lyrics were written by Novelle Richards, a poet and author. Both song and lyrics were adopted as the national anthem in 1967. After full independence, the first eight lines of the anthem were changed in 1981 to include Barbuda.

Fair Antigua and Barbuda
We thy sons and daughters stand,
Strong and firm in peace or danger
To safeguard our native land.
We commit ourselves to building
A true nation, brave and free.
Ever striving, ever seeking,
Dwell in love and unity.
Raise the standard!
Raise it boldly!
Answer now to duty's call
To the service of thy country,
Sparing nothing, giving all;

Gird your loins and join the battle
'Gainst fear, hate and poverty
Each endeavouring, all achieving,
Live in peace where man is free.
God of nations, let Thy blessings
Fall upon this land of ours
Rain and sunshine ever sending,
Fill her fields with crops and flowers;
We her children do implore thee,
Give us strength, faith, loyalty,
Never failing, all enduring
To defend her liberty.

THE ANTIGUA AND BARBUDA DEFENSE FORCE

The defense force was formed after independence. Prior to that it was a volunteer force called the Antigua Defense Force. Its main purpose was to protect the interest of the sugarcane planters. Today, the Antigua Barbuda Defense Force protects the civilian population of the country. Some of its duties are to prevent smuggling, provide internal security, and conduct search and rescue operations.

In 2004 Antigua had a defense force of 170 men, with 125 in the army and the other 45 in the navy. The defense force comes under the Ministry of Defense, which also includes the coast guard. The headquarters of the defense force is located near Parham at Camp Blizard, which used to be a U.S. Navy facility.

The Antigua and Barbuda Defense Force on parade. Antigua and Barbuda established its own defense force after gaining independence from the British.

ECONOMY

ANTIGUA'S PAST ECONOMY WAS BASED on agriculture, mainly the cultivation of sugarcane. This has changed tremendously over the last few decades. Although many Antiguans continue to find employment in the agricultural sector, the major source of income in Antigua is tourism, which contributes more than 60 percent to the overall gross domestic product (GDP) of the country.

In 2004 Antigua and Barbuda's gross national income was more than $815 million, which means that the average yearly income was $10,185. The average income of Antiguans and Barbudans has increased steadily since 2001. Antigua and Barbuda has some of the lowest unemployment rates among the Caribbean countries.

ECONOMIC DIVISIONS

The economy of Antigua and Barbuda is divided primarily into three sectors: agriculture, manufacturing, and services. About 25 percent of the population of Antigua and Barbuda is employed in agriculture. Most of the crops are not grown for export, but instead are grown to feed the populace on the two islands.

Because of Antigua and Barbuda's Caribbean climate, a wide variety of fruits are grown there. The crops grown today, mostly in the southern part of Antigua, are mainly cucumbers, coconuts, mangoes, melons, pumpkins, limes, Antiguan black pineapples, and sweet potatoes. Antigua's most important root crop is the sweet potato. It is included in many Antiguan recipes. Some crops grown on Barbuda are peanuts, corn, melons, and coconuts.

Above: **A woman selling hats and bags at her stall.**

Opposite: **Tourists buying refreshments from a roadside stand. The bulk of Antigua and Barbuda's income comes from tourism.**

Other fruits and vegetables grown are passion fruit, bananas, cantaloupes, papayas, avocados, and cherries. Fruits grow in abundance in the wild, and dates and sea grapes can be found hanging from trees and bushes. Other vegetables grown locally are carrots, cabbage, squash, and a variety of peppers.

Even though wild sugarcane can be found throughout the island, it is no longer cultivated as a crop. However, some industrious vendors will chop the canes down, peel off the thick bark, and chop the cane into small pieces. These are then put into a plastic bag and sold along the road or in the markets.

Most farmers in Antigua and Barbuda are small producers. They are the backbone of the food economy. These farmers sell their

Patches of crop fields can be found all over Antigua and Barbuda. These allow for a wide variety of locally grown produce to be sold at the markets.

fruits and vegetables through an organization called the Central Marketing Corporation.

Crab, shrimp, and lobster farming also fall under the heading of agriculture. This type of farming was further encouraged by the Ministry of Agriculture, Lands, and Fisheries, and new projects were implemented in the 1990s to increase it.

Agriculture on Antigua and Barbuda has one major obstacle: an insufficient water supply. To remove reliance on rainfall, the government installed a desalination plant that holds 2 million gallons of water per day on the northeast coast of Antigua, thus creating a continuous supply of water from the Caribbean Sea. Barbuda also has a desalination plant in addition to many wells, some of which were dug during the time of Codrington.

The surrounding seas of Antigua and Barbuda teem with fish, which is a staple food on the islands.

Wild donkeys can be seen roaming freely in less populated areas of Antigua and Barbuda.

DOMESTIC ANIMALS

Antigua and Barbuda is also home to several different types of livestock, such as cattle, pigs, goats, and sheep. Even today, it is not uncommon to see herds of goats and sheep wandering along the roads in the countryside. Drivers must be especially careful not to hit them while coming around sharp curves.

It is very difficult to tell the goats and sheep apart, since the sheep in Antigua do not have thick wool. There is a local saying that "goat's tails are up and sheep tails are down."

In Barbuda there are many wild donkeys. They are seen walking along the road, grazing in the brush, or heard braying during the night.

These wild donkeys are descendants of tame donkeys that were used for transportation many years ago. They have long since been replaced by cars and bicycles. Once these new forms of transport arrived in Barbuda, the donkeys were left to fend for themselves.

MANUFACTURING

The manufacturing sector does not have a significant presence on the two islands. Garments, paints, furniture, food, and beverages are produced on a small-scale in Antigua. Assembly lines that put together electrical components and household appliances can also be found there. Many of these factories are located on Factory Road, close to the international airport.

SERVICES

Services constitute the largest sector and include construction services, financial services, and most importantly, tourism. However, because of

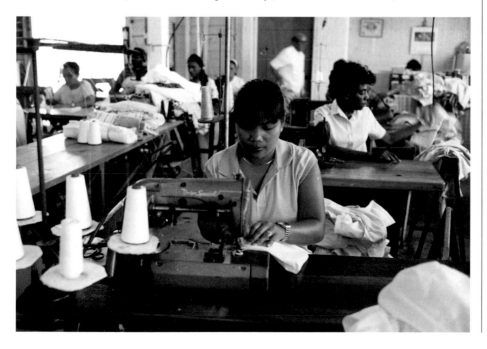

There are a number of manufacturers that operate on a small-scale on Antigua and Barbuda.

past hurricanes and terror attacks in the United States, the number of tourists to Antigua has fluctuated. In 2004, the number of tourists in Antigua reached 768,209. These tourists were primarily from Europe, the United States, Canada, and other Caribbean countries.

Tourists stay on the islands for a vacation or arrive on cruise ships. They snorkel in the crystal clear waters, explore pristine white sand beaches, or shop in Saint John's.

Falmouth Harbor, English Harbor, and Jolly Harbor are another source of income for the country. Huge yachts dock in these harbors, which are set up like small towns with facilities for fresh water, electricity, diesel, restaurants, and shops. Around the months of June and July, just about all of the yachts anchored in these harbors leave Antigua. During the hurricane season the harbors are almost completely empty.

Beautiful resorts have been constructed along the shore lines of the two islands, making construction the second most important industry to the economy. Programs for foreign investment in new hotels and resorts have been established by the government. Local resorts are also encouraged to institute social programs in the area, such as further education assistance for needy children.

The financial services available in Antigua and Barbuda include offshore banking. This type of banking allows a person or a corporation to set up a bank account where the information of its contents and transactions of are kept confidential.

TRADING PARTNERS

Antigua and Barbuda is a member of the Caribbean Community and Common Market organisation, or CARICOM. Member countries include Antigua and Barbuda, the Bahamas, Barbados, Belize, Dominica, Grenada,

Guyana, Haiti, Jamaica, Montserrat, Saint Lucia, Saint Kitts and Nevis, Saint Vincent and the Grenadines, Suriname, and Trinidad and Tobago. The members of CARICOM are Antigua's principal trading partners, as well as the United States, Canada, France, and England.

In the past Antigua and Barbuda was eligible for the U.S. General System of Preferences. This system was created to increase economic growth in developing countries. Beneficiary countries were provided with duty-free entry into the United States for over 4,650 products. This program began in 1976 and has been continually renewed up until 2004, when Antigua and Barbuda was deemed too wealthy to continue to be part of the program. As a result, the country was removed from the list of beneficiaries.

In 2004 Antigua and Barbuda exported $689 million worth of products and goods but imported $735 million worth. Some products that were exported were food and live animals, iron and steel, and telecommunications equipment. A few of the products imported were vegetables and fruit, meat, tobacco, and mineral fuels such as lubricants. Barbuda's two main exports are sand and lobster.

BANKING

The central bank is located in Saint Kitts and is called The East Caribbean Central Bank. Two banks, the Antigua Commercial Bank and the Antigua Barbuda Investment Bank, are locally owned. In addition, there are several international banks doing business in the country.

Legislation was passed in 1982 under the International Business Corporations Act to allow offshore banking. In 2002 there were 21 offshore banks operating in Antigua.

The activities of these banks are closely regulated by a statutory commission, or a commission established by a legislative body called the Financial Services Regulatory Commission.

To prevent money laundering, offshore banking has a strong "know your customer" requirement. No anonymous accounts can be set up. In addition, a bank account application requires evidence of identity, place of residence, and complete disclosure of beneficiaries of the account, and does not allow any cash deposits.

It is not uncommon to see mules and donkeys used as a mode of transportation on the roads of Antigua and Barbuda.

TRANSPORTATION

Antigua and Barbuda has a total of 239 miles (384 km) of main roads and 485 miles (781 km) of secondary roads. Getting around Antigua is relatively easy because many of its roads are paved. Tourists' buses speed along these roads, taking cruise ship passengers to day excursions such as diving with the rays. Service vehicles, such as heavy construction trucks and phone repair vehicles are also able to maneuver around the island easily. Traffic can get quite heavy in Saint John's during rush hour. But it lightens up closer to the outer villages.

Occasionally, a man may be spotted riding a mule or boys riding a horse along the road. Even though this form of transportation is not common, it still exists.

In Barbuda there are no paved roads. All of the roads are made of dirt, gravel, or crushed coral. It is not uncommon to see Barbudans driving vehicles with four-wheel drive to navigate its rough road system.

Tourists arrive in Antigua at the only international airport, which is located several miles outside of Saint John's, called the V.C. Bird International Airport. Several major airlines fly to Antigua from Europe, Canada, the United States, and the Caribbean. A smaller airport is located in Barbuda. Tourists may also arrive by cruise ship, which usually dock near Redcliffe and Heritage Quay in Saint John's. Cargo ships dock in Deepwater Harbor, farther away from Saint John's, next to a dockyard filled with cargo containers.

COMMUNICATION

The future progress of Antigua in the international business world depends heavily on communication services. Tourism and international banking are two such important industries that benefit from these facilities.

Communication services are very well developed in Antigua and Barbuda. Landline phones and cellular phones can be found throughout the two islands. In 2001, 62,300 people had landline phones. In 2002 there were 38,200 cellular phone subscribers, as well as 10,000 Internet users. A company called Cable and Wireless is one of the largest service providers in the country.

ENVIRONMENT

THE LANDSCAPE OF ANTIGUA is mostly covered with shrubs and acacia trees, whereas the land on Barbuda is covered with a dry savannah of cacti and thorn bushes. Antigua was one of the most heavily forested islands in the Caribbean in the 17th century. Much of this forest was cleared to provide wood for constructing buildings and ships and to plant sugarcane. Even though most of the forests are gone, Antigua remains green and colorful.

Indigenous animals mix with animals from faraway countries, making a very unique environment. Individual Antiguans, with government support, have made a huge effort to maintain the natural wonders that exist in this island country. One such success story is the Hawksbill turtle.

Above: **Devil's Bridge Peninsula. Much of Antigua and Barbuda is shrub—the result of heavy deforestation during the colonial era.**

Opposite: **Wallings Forest consists of the dense forestation that used to cover significant areas of Antigua and Barbuda.**

JUMBY BAY HAWKSBILL CONSERVATION PROJECT

This project began in 1986 when an Antiguan, John Fuller, observed that huge concentrations of Hawksbills were nesting on a small sandy beach on Long Island, a small island off Antigua. Fuller contacted a well-known sea turtle expert, Dr. Jim Richardson. From Fuller's description Richardson realized that the Hawksbill nesting ground was unique. After further study it was discovered that the Hawksbill nesting area was one of the largest in the world.

This environmentally valuable region has been protected since 1989. Part of the conservation project includes having two biologists assigned to the area continuously between June and November. Their job is to patrol the almost half a mile (0.8 km) of beach every hour during the night for 153 nights. These biologists look for tracks made in the sand by female Hawksbills that have come ashore to lay their eggs.

The Hawksbill turtle is the subject of intense conservation efforts in Antigua and Barbuda.

Once the female begins laying her eggs, she goes into a sort of trancelike state. During this time the biologists can do a number of tests, which they document. These tests include measuring her shell, counting how many eggs she has laid, and giving her an identification tag. If she already has a tag, it is noted. All of this data tracks the population of the Hawksbill turtle in Jumby Bay. Unfortunately, very few hatchlings survive. On average about 1 in 1,000 to 3,000 hatchlings make it to reproductive age.

Viewing the turtle nests and turtles is not restricted to the turtle researchers and biologists. Guests staying at Jumby Bay Resort are also invited. In addition, the Antigua and Barbuda Environmental Awareness Group supports outings for others to come and view the nesting areas. This extensive project is supported and funded by the Jumby Bay Island Company and Cable and Wireless, Antigua.

SAVING THE ANTIGUAN RACER

The rarest snake in the world is only found on Antigua. This gentle, gray-brown snake is called the Antiguan Racer. Kevel Lindsay, who worked for the Island Resources Foundation, and Mark Day, who worked for Fauna and Flora International, were both snake fans. Kevel was interested in the Antiguan Racer since high school. He asked about the snake and was told that they were found on Great Bird Island in the past.

In 1995 Lindsey and Day decided to go to Great Bird Island to see if they could find the Antiguan Racer. They searched for hours and could not find the small snake. Just as they were about to give up, someone on the search team found one. After the team's discovery the Antiguan Forestry Unit gave permission to conduct a survey that lasted for six weeks. The results showed there were only 50 racers left, so the Antiguan Racer Conservation Project was formed.

To save the Antiguan Racer from extinction, the conservation project focused worldwide attention on this endangered snake. It did this in a variety of ways, such as establishing breeding programs of racers, changing public attitudes toward snakes, tagging and studying racers, and securing the government's agreement to save the snake.

Another barrier against saving the snake was its enemy, the rat. The rate ate the eggs of the Antiguan racer, which had been brought to the island by man. To handle this problem a rat eradication expert was called. He suggested using a poison called Klerat. This poison kills rats without hurting other animals. With the careful use of this poison, the rats were completely cleared from the island. Today, because of these local efforts, the Antiguan Racer continues to live on Great Bird Island.

Hawksbill turtle hatchlings heading out to sea. Despite their large numbers, few actually make it to maturity.

This project is very important for this critically endangered species. The Hawksbill has reached this status through a loss of nesting and feeding habits, pollution, egg-collection, and development on coastlines. In addition, these turtles are still killed for their shells, even though they have a protected status.

The indigenous Hawksbill turtle is the national creature of the sea for Antigua. It was once hunted for its beautiful tortoiseshell. These shells were used to make combs, spectacle frames, decorative fans, and cigarette boxes, but today they are protected. The shell is about 3 feet (.91 m) long and weighs about 175 pounds (80 kg). They can live up to 50 years. Hawksbill turtles do not migrate regularly like some turtles, but appear to stay in the same place. They can be found while snorkeling on the coral reefs. Antigua boosts the largest nesting area of Hawksbills in the Caribbean, with about 500 Hawksbill's nests and around 18,000 hatchlings produced in a year.

ISLAND RESOURCES FOUNDATION

This 27-year-old foundation specializes in assisting governments and private nonprofit environmental organizations of small tropical islands. It does this by providing them with development and environmental planning. Its main headquarters is located in St. Thomas, U.S. Virgin Islands, but it also has branch offices in Washington, DC, and Saint John's, Antigua.

The main objective of this organization is to provide species protection of the coastal areas through various programs that it oversees in coordination with the local government.

To date this foundation has been engaged in over 150 projects. Some of the projects it has been involved in with Antigua and Barbuda include: protecting seabirds and native snakes, establishing the Bird Island Marine Reserve and Wildlife Sanctuary, surveying or examining nine reef sites and providing recommendations for continuing marine management, establishing a project to preserve Barbuda's Codrington Lagoon or Frigate Bird Sanctuary, and also participating in a funded project to map the wetlands of Antigua.

NATIONAL PARKS, PROTECTED AREAS, AND NATURAL REFUGES

One such natural refuge for a variety of endangered species is Great Bird Island. This very small island is about 1.9 miles (3 km) northeast of

The reefs of Antigua and Barbuda abound with rich biodiversity.

Antigua. Sailors named it Great Bird Island years ago because of the huge amount of birds they found living there. Endangered species found there are brown pelicans, West Indian Whistling-ducks, Red-billed Tropicbirds, and a rare lizard. It is also the only place in the world where you can see the Antiguan Racer snake in the wild.

FRIGATE BIRD SANCTUARY Codrington Lagoon on Barbuda is where the national bird of Antigua, the frigate bird, lives in a protected sanctuary. There are five species of frigate birds worldwide. Two of these species are endangered. However, the one found on Barbuda, the magnificent frigate bird, is not. Even so, it is important to protect these huge birds.

This male frigate bird blows his breast up like a balloon to attract females.

Codrington Lagoon in Barbuda is the largest nesting colony of frigate birds in the world. It is also one of the world's most important areas for preserving these birds as there are few predators in this area. Thousands of frigate birds breed and nest there from September to April. Even though there are many frigate birds in one place, they are amazingly quiet, making only soft twittering noises.

Both male and female birds are shiny black. The main difference between the two is that the female has a white breast and the male has a bright red breast. During mating, to attract a female, the male expands his red breast like a balloon and thumps it with his beak, making a soft drumming noise. The female lays only one egg on a nest built on mangrove trees. Once hatched, the baby chicks are covered in white down, much like a cotton ball. The chick depends on its parents for up to 11 months before it will fend for itself.

Frigate birds can be found at the bird sanctuary on Barbuda—a draw for bird enthusiasts.

The wings on these large birds are a little over 7-feet (2.1-m) long from tip to tip, and they weigh about 3 pounds (1.4 kg) each. Their diet consists mostly of fish that they often steal from other birds.

These huge birds glide with the air currents. Like most birds, Frigate birds are excellent at flying. However, they swim and walk with much difficulty because of their weak legs. If a frigate accidentally lands in the water, scientists have observed other frigates coming to the drowning bird's rescue and pulling it safely to shore.

WALLINGS FOREST AND RESERVOIR On the southwest side of Antigua is Wallings Forest and Reservoir. Originally, Wallings was a water reservoir designed to hold up to 13 million gallons of water. Because the area was used as a reservoir, its forests were completely stripped by 1900. Later in 1915, tree seeds were planted on a 13-acre (5.5-ha) section of Wallings to reforest the area. Some of the trees that can be found at Wallings today are locusts, ironwoods, mahoes, mangoes, white cedars, mahoganies, and Spanish oaks.

In the 1990s Wallings Forest and Reservoir was established as a conservation area. This was done by the Antigua and Barbuda government with the assistance of the Island Resources Foundation.

DEVIL'S BRIDGE PARK

In the 1950s the northeastern point of Antigua was officially made a national park. It is known as Devil's Bridge Park because of the natural arch found there, which has been carved by years of seawater erosion. This soft and hard limestone bridge is about 30 feet (9 m) long and 12 feet (3.6 m) high.

ENVIRONMENTAL EDUCATION

Antigua and Barbuda is a relatively new nation and, as a result, environmental programs have been implemented to educate its citizens. Environmental education has become a useful tool in preserving Antigua and Barbuda's natural wonders. Environmental awareness campaigns feature announcements on television telling the public not to litter. There is also a fine of up to $500 for anyone caught littering. In addition, the Environment Division has recently held many competitions to increase public awareness about environmental conservation. These competitions include an environmental cartoon contest, a village beautification competition, and a recyclable material craft competition. Antigua and Barbuda Agriculture Forum for Youth was also organized for young adults aged 16 to 35. Its purpose is to build local leadership, encourage and facilitate the efforts of young people to grow and market food, and conserve local resources. Grants of up to $500 Eastern Caribbean dollars are also issued to qualifying students to assist with their environmental research and any supplies or training they may need.

Strong waves cause water to spout through the holes of the infamous Devil's Bridge.

67

ANTIGUANS & BARBUDANS

THOUSANDS OF AFRICAN SLAVES were brought into Antigua and Barbuda from West Africa between the 17th and 18th centuries. Once independence was achieved, the majority of the population that remained on the two islands was of African descent.

FROM SLAVES TO ANTIGUANS

The bonds of slavery were never accepted by the enslaved Africans. There are accounts of slave runaways starting in 1680. African slaves began organizing revolts against their white masters as early as 1687. Stories of runaway camps established on Boggy Peak, rewards for captured runaway slaves, and occasional revolts continued through the late 17th and early 18th centuries. But the largest planned rebellion recorded was in 1736.

Left: **Antiguans and Barbudans lead a typically modern lifestyle.**

Opposite: **The majority of Antiguans and Barbudans are descendents of black Africans.**

FATHER OF THE NATION

Born on the outskirts of Saint John's on December 9, 1909, Vere Cornwall Bird was raised in abject poverty. His parents were Barbara Edghill and Theophilus Bird. Vere was the fourth out of five children. He attended Saint John's Boys' School where he received an elementary school education.

When he was older he joined the Salvation Army and was sent to Jamaica to receive training. While there he visited many other Caribbean islands. He was deeply touched by the extreme poverty he witnessed in the area and decided to make it his life mission to change this condition.

In 1939 V.C. Bird was selected to attend a historical meeting in Antigua and Barbuda. Sir Walter Citrine, a member of the Royal Commission, called the meeting. He was sent to the area to investigate what was causing the workers' riots. The outcome of this meeting was the formation of the Antigua Trades and Labor Union. V. C. Bird became an executive member of the newly established union. By 1942 he had become the union's second president.

After the labor union was created, it immediately won several victories that began establishing workers' rights. Even though there was progress, the political power of Antigua was still held by the plantation owners. The members of the Antigua Trades and Labor Union soon realized that in order to gain control for the workers, the union would have to hold political power. As a result, the ALP was established in 1946. V. C. Bird was encouraged to run for election to become a member of the Legislative Council, which he won in 1946.

As Antigua began to gain more independence from Great Britain, V. C. Bird was appointed as the first chief minister of Antigua and Barbuda in 1960. This position helped Bird shape the political structure of the country.

Eleven years later he formed the ALP. He was elected the first prime minister of Antigua after its complete independence was established. He served as prime minister of Antigua and Barbuda for 13 years.

In 1994 V. C. Bird was named the first national hero. After a prolonged illness he passed away on June 28, 1999 when he was 89 years old.

Three slaves formulated a plan in a ravine or gully called Stony Hill Gully. Their names were Prince Klaas, Tomboy, and Hercules. Their plan was to invade a ball held in honor of George II's coronation at Christopher Dunbar's house in Saint John's. The majority of plantation owners were going to attend. Three groups of 350 slaves were to enter Saint John's during the ball and kill all the whites. The uprising was never executed, as the ball was postponed and a slave named Johnny told the authorities about the plan. The three ringleaders were executed at the market. In addition, many other slaves were put to death.

Barbudan slaves were a bit freer because they could farm their own plots of land and worked as herdsmen, hunters, and fishermen. They were also taught to become craftsmen, working as tanners, shoemakers, and carpenters. Even though they were considered happier than the slaves on Antigua, there was still much anger and dissatisfaction because of their status as slaves.

The first slave uprising was recorded in 1741 on Barbuda and was initiated because of a cruel manager. The slaves killed several cows and damaged some of Codrington's equipment. Several uprisings occurred throughout the years, but the most serious one was between 1834 and 1835. All Barbudans were told that they were to be shipped to Antigua to work on Codrington's plantations. This caused intense anger. Troops had to be sent from Antigua to stop the revolt. Another issue that instigated this revolt was the British parliament's failure to name Barbudans in the Slavery Emancipation Act of 1834. Instead, Barbudan slaves had to take steps to free themselves.

Even though slavery was abolished in 1834, former slaves continued working for plantation owners.

Additional developments continued that began to form the current country of Antigua and Barbuda today. In 1860 the British Parliament made

Barbuda a dependency of Antigua. Even so, the government of Antigua did not set up an administration for Barbuda because it was still leased to the Codringtons. By 1870 the black Barbudans began complaining of their treatment on the island. The governor of Antigua canceled Codrington's lease to Barbuda, which ended their long association with the island.

Disputes with the Antiguan government and the black Barbudans as to property ownership began in 1904. Barbudans considered all land to be communal property, whereas the government wanted them to pay rent. Overall, Barbudans ignored any demands for rent payment.

In 1915, a struggle with the Antiguan government took place. A shipwreck was found off the coast of Barbuda, and the locals began to salvage its cargo and equipment. A warden of the Antiguan government arrived, demanding 10 percent of the salvage. Barbudans believed that when the Codringtons left the island, they had also left the Barbudans the right to all salvage. The the Barbudans burned the warden's boat and cart in response to his demands. The governor of Antigua threatened to enforce rent payments if the culprits were not found. In the end, the matter was left unresolved.

In contrast, by 1918, freed black Antiguans were becoming more educated and started understanding their rights. The black workers on

Antigua began demanding an honest pay for their work. It was widely known that the local planters were getting high prices for their crops. But the profits were not passed on, and these same planters still paid the black workers very low wages.

Tempers flared and a riot followed. Dissatisfied workers threw rocks at the police and defense force. Shots were fired back. By the end of the riot, two people were dead and 13 had been injured. The riot, however, proved fruitless as there was no rise in wages for black Antiguans. Many became homeless and were beggars.

Labor conditions were extremely poor until the founding of the Antigua Trades and Labor Union in 1939. This labor union was established to ensure that workers' rights would be protected. In addition, the union became a bargaining organization between plantation owners and workers. Black Antiguan workers wasted no time in joining the new union.

AFRICAN INFLUENCES

Because the majority of Antiguans have links with African ancestors, many of the customs from West Africa were handed down from generation to generation. One of these customs is the art of healing from wild plants, also known as bush plant healing. It began during the time of slavery.

ETHNIC STATISTICS

About 94 percent of the population in Antigua and Barbuda consists of descendants of black Africans. Mulattoes, or people who have mixed parents such as one black parent and one white, make up about 3.7 percent. Whites make up around 2.4 percent of the population. The rest of the population is British, Arab, and Portuguese.

Because the slaves had little access to doctors, they experimented with the local plants and herbs to cure illnesses and heal the sick. This type of alternative medicine is still in practice today by the older generation but is not being passed on to the younger generation due to a lack of interest.

Many foods and dishes were brought to Antigua and Barbuda by the slaves. Some of these foods are bonavista beans, okra, and eggplants. Some African dish names are fungee, seasoned rice, goatwater, and black pudding, a type of sausage made with cooked rice that is mixed with animal blood and seasoning; it is then stuffed into a pig or cow gut and cooked until tender.

Superstitions have also carried down through the ages. Obeah was brought from West Africa. It is an animistic belief, which invokes spiritual beings and is similar to voodoo. Obeah believes in spirits called *jumbies,* which are mischievous spirits that live in the bush or in graveyards. Preparing herbal potions is another important part of Obeah, as well as making doll images of a person and sticking pins in the doll to cause pain to that person.

Even though Obeah was declared illegal—as it was harmful to others and has even been known to kill people—it is still sometimes practiced by people who have come to Antigua from other countries, such as Haiti, Guadeloupe, and Dominica. However, the majority of the population in Antigua and Barbuda is Christian.

African names can still be found in Antigua today. Names such as Ogwambi, Nkosi, and Malika are listed in the telephone book.

ETHNIC MINORITIES

Descendants of British colonial settlers, mulattoes, Portuguese laborers, and Lebanese and Syrian traders all live on Antigua and Barbuda today.

The Portuguese came to Antigua as workers in the 19th century. These small business owners are considered the middle class of Antigua and Barbuda. Traders from the Middle East established themselves in Antiguan and Barbudan society in the 20th century. Even though individuals in this group are from many different countries, they are usually referred to as Syrians.

Because of the appealing climate and beautiful beaches, Antigua and Barbuda has recently attracted North Americans, Europeans, and Asians who want to make the island their home. Included in this recent group of immigrants are sailors, artists, and businessmen.

Spanish-speaking immigrants have also started immigrating to Antigua and Barbuda. They come from such countries as the Dominican Republic, Guyana, and Dominica.

The prisine waters and wonderful warm weather of Antigua and Barbuda are some of the draws for immigrants to the country.

LIFESTYLE

MOST CARIBBEAN COUNTRIES HAVE a laid-back lifestyle. Antigua and Barbuda is no exception. The majority of people live in small villages where everyone knows each other's business. On Barbuda it is thought that everyone is somehow related.

Time moves slowly as people congregate on their porches or on the street to visit, have a barbecue, or play a game of cards. Wandering domesticated animals are also part of village life. Roosters scratch dirt, while goats and sheep bleat and wander from place to place.

CLOTHING

Clothing in Antigua and Barbuda has changed throughout the years. Today, Antiguan and Barbudans wear Western-style clothing appropriate for tropical weather. Men usually wear blue jeans or cotton pants with T-shirts or button-down shirts. Baseball caps are sometimes worn to shade them from the sun. When it is hot, men may also wear shorts.

Women wear fabric dresses or skirts with loose fitting tops. They also wear cotton pants, cropped pants, and blue jeans. One tradition that has lasted from the days of slavery is women using head ties. These ties are usually colorful and are wrapped around the head. This tradition can be traced back to Antigua and Barbuda's African roots.

Men and women involved in business might wear Western business suits. Women usually wear skirts with matching jackets. Stockings or panty hose are not normally worn.

During festivals, costumes are extremely elaborate and colorful for both men and women. The colors gold, orange, yellow, pink, purple, blue, and green are common. Women sometimes wear tall headdresses and ornaments attached to their backs.

Opposite: **Schoolchildren and pedestrians walk along the streets of Saint John's.**

When children attend school they must wear uniforms. Each school has a different uniform. Girls might wear skirts with blouses, or dresses with white and blue checks. Boys wear slacks or shorts with matching shirts, such as a pair of black pants with a white shirt. When boys graduate to secondary school, they have to wear a tie. All school uniforms are manufactured in Antigua.

HOMES

The majority of houses in Antigua and Barbuda are constructed out of concrete or wood. However, some are built using the local green limestone. Most have two bedrooms, a living room, a kitchen, and a bathroom; even so, some homes are very small and often consist of only one room that is 6 feet (1.83 m) by 10 feet (3.05 m). The majority of people have indoor plumbing as well as electricity.

Houses are often painted in bright, cheerful colors, such as pink, yellow, or peach and white. Some houses are multicolored with red roofs, yellow siding, purple windows, and blue trim. Even local churches are colorful; examples are a peach-colored Catholic church and a yellow Baptist church.

FAMILY LIFE

Couples are united in three different ways: they are legally married, they are unmarried but live together, or they are joined in a union where the man and woman have children together, but live in different locations; this is called a visiting union. It is not uncommon for a man in Antigua to have two or three families living in different locations. This may stem from past customs of African slaves fathering many

NATIONAL CLOTHING OF ANTIGUA AND BARBUDA

A national Antiguan dress competition was held in May 1992. The purpose of the competition, ran by the Library Fundraising Committee, was to raise funds for a new public library in Barbuda. Designs needed to be submitted for both men and women. Heather Doram, an Antiguan, won the competition. Her design was based on clothing worn by cake makers and market vendors in Antigua around 1834.

Madras fabric was selected to make the costume. Madras is a cotton cloth that has stripes or is plaid. The colors of red, gold, and green were selected for the madras of the Antiguan national clothing.

The female costume consists of a head tie, a dress with puff sleeves that is gathered at the waist and covered with a stiff white cotton apron. The male costume consists of a straw hat, a starched white shirt that is covered with a waistcoat made of madras, black pants and shoes, and white socks. The national costume is worn to celebrate "Heritage Day" in October.

children out of wedlock. Around 60 years ago it was recorded that one man fathered about 35 children with a variety of women.

Because of economic or other factors, children may or may not be raised by their parents; instead, they may be raised in a variety of households or with relatives. The common law in Antigua and Barbuda identifies that children should receive care and attention by their parents.

Under Antiguan and Barbudan law, there is little difference between the children born out of wedlock and legitimate children. In 1987 a law called the Status of Children Act was passed, making it illegal to discriminate against illegitimate children, especially concerning inheritance. In addition, the father of the child, whether married or not, is responsible for paying child support. Parliament is currently considering whether or not child support should be taken out of the father's paycheck.

VILLAGE LIFE

The majority of people in Antigua and Barbuda live in villages. Each village has a police station, a church, usually with an attached cemetery, a grocery store, retail stores, a primary school, a secondary school, and a medical clinic that is staffed every day of the week.

Farming and fishing are common in village life. Fishermen use nets, metal cages, and fishing poles to catch fish. They may also put on a snorkel mask, bend over the side of the boat, and take a look around in the water to spot conchs or lobsters. Crops such as fruits and vegetables are grown either to be sold to hotels, Saint John's public market, or for personal consumption.

MARRIAGE

Meeting future spouses in Antigua and Barbuda could be as simple as knowing them from childhood, going to a party, or meeting them at school. Even though not all Antiguan and Barbudans get married before having children, some do. Their weddings are very similar to Western-style weddings.

One tradition is that prior to the wedding, the bride may receive gifts from family members that follow an old saying: something old, something new, something borrowed, and something blue.

Children are an important part of Antiguan and Barbudan society.

The bride wears a white, sometimes ornate dress, and the groom may wear a nice suit consisting of trousers and a jacket. The ceremony is usually held in a traditional Christian church and presided over by a minister. It is followed by a reception where a cake may be cut and speeches are made to the newly married couple. Antiguan wedding cake is usually a fruitcake, so it is dark and almost black in color. Sometimes, the bride and groom will freeze the top tier of their wedding cake to eat on their first anniversary. Civil weddings are also done in Antigua without as much fanfare and expense.

FUNERALS

Antiguan funerals usually begin with a church service, and speeches are made to honor the recently deceased. The funeral party then proceeds to the cemetery where the casket is buried.

Some of the older members of the community follow the old tradition of observing a wake, which includes recounting stories of the deceased's life, singing, and praying with family members and close friends. The wake before the funeral is usually very glum. A wake is an all-night vigil over the deceased before the burial. In the past this all-night watch took place in the house of the deceased. Historically, wakes were held with the hope that the deceased might wake up or come back to life. Today, they are usually held in a funeral home.

In modern times it has become a time to mourn and be consoled by friends and family before the burial.

There are also wakes that take place after the funeral. A wider circle of friends are invited, and this wake tends to be more festive. Food is served while memories of the deceased are recounted.

A holiday for Catholics is All Souls' Day, which is celebrated on November 2 in Antigua. Flowers and candles are left at the graves of loved ones.

THE ROLE OF WOMEN

Women on this twin-island country have access to education at all levels. As a result, they are welcomed in any field they wish to pursue. Today, more and more women are getting educated and finding work in many different types of occupations.

Organizations for women, such as the Professional Organization for Women of Antigua, have been formed to assist women in their careers. Throughout the last couple of decades, women have begun to hold political positions such as senator and Speaker of the House of Representatives, serve on the Board of Education, run the National Parks Foundation, act as the chief medical officer, and work in various government ministries such as Justice and Legal Affairs.

Business is another area where women are becoming active. Women merchants are not uncommon, especially in the fabric industry. One woman was a powerful moneylender and another became the general manager in the Royal Bank of Canada.

Women have become involved in the arts by designing costumes, acting, dancing to calypso, and creative writing. One woman even held the position of director of culture in the government.

EDUCATION

The Antiguan and Barbudan educational system is based on the British system. It is a system with three tiers: primary, secondary, and tertiary. Education is free and compulsory up to the age of 16.

Each grade level is called a form. Prior to primary education there are several preschools or preprimary schools for children ages 3 to 6. All preschools are privately owned. However, some government schools have begun to offer kindergarten classes.

Primary education is for children ages 6 and up. Once primary education is completed, each student must take a national Primary School Examination to be able to pass on to secondary school. This test is taken at the age of 11 or 12, depending on the student's abilities.

In school 10-year-old children learn such topics as: social studies, which includes ecotourism, family, and kindness to pets; math, which includes addition, fractions, decimals, and percentages; and Drug Abuse Resistance Education.

Secondary school in Antigua and Barbuda last from four to five years. The age of secondary school students range from 11 or 12 to 18 years old. These students must complete five forms. Once the forms are complete, the students must take the examinations of the Caribbean Examination Council, which, upon completion, is equivalent to earning a North American high school diploma.

The compulsory primary school education instituted by the government of Antigua and Barbuda has resulted in a high literacy rate of approximately 90 percent.

COLLEGES AND SPECIAL EDUCATION Even though very few Antiguans and Barbudans actually make it to the tertiary level of education, there are four tertiary, or college-level schools in Antigua. They are the Antigua State College, the University of the West Indies School of Continuing Studies, the Antigua and Barbuda Hospitality Training Institute, and the Antigua and Barbuda International Institute of Technology.

Antigua State College was established in 1977. It offers a two-year program for several fields, such as teacher training, business, commerce, nursing, pharmacy, and engineering.

The University of the West Indies, based in Saint Augustine, Trinidad, is a comprehensive university that also offers graduate programs. This university has a continuing-education campus located in Antigua.

The Antigua and Barbuda Hospitality Training Institute provides training to those students wanting to work in the hospitality industry. Topics such as the culinary arts and hotel management are taught there.

Students can further their education on computer technologies at the Antigua and Barbuda International Institute of Technology. Networking, Internet, and software training are provided at this school.

PUBLIC TRANSPORTATION

There are two types of public transportation: buses and taxis. The majority of Antiguans take public buses, which begin their journey from the bus station next to the public market in Saint John's. Each bus is labeled with its destination. There is no timetable for bus departure and arrival. The bus driver simply leaves when the bus is full. This type of system makes it a challenge for people waiting at bus stops throughout the island. The buses usually run until 7:00 or 8:00 P.M. unless there is a big show in town. On Barbuda there are no public buses.

Taxis are very expensive because all gas in the country is imported from Venezuela. Throughout Antigua there are many gas stations, but on Barbuda, there is only one. The way to identify whether or not a van is a bus or a taxi is by its license plate. The license plate on a bus license begins with the letters B, U, and S, and then a number, whereas a taxi's starts with the letters T, X, and then a number.

MEDICAL CARE

Antigua and Barbuda have a well-developed health care system. To make it affordable the Medical Benefits Scheme was established. Chronic illnesses and diseases found to occur in the area are covered by this scheme. These include diabetes, asthma, and heart disease.

Throughout the country there are 26 health centers that provide general health care, as well as prenatal and postnatal care of mothers. The health of children is extremely important to the government of Antigua. Vaccinations against childhood diseases are mandatory. When a child begins school, the parents must provide records of the vaccinations that the child has gotten.

In addition, there is a hospital in Antigua that provides surgery, and many private health-care facilities, including laboratories. There is another hospital on Barbuda, but it is very small. It has 10 beds. The hospital has no surgery facilities and has only recently acquired an x-ray machine. Hence, if people need surgery of any kind, they must be flown to Antigua. The hospital in Barbuda is mainly used for childbirth and for the dispensation of medication by a qualified doctor and pharmacist.

RELIGION

THE CONSTITUTION OF ANTIGUA AND BARBUDA clearly states that freedom of religion is a vital right of the country's citizens.

Because of colonization by the British, Christianity has had a strong hold on the society up to modern times. On Sunday most Christian churches on the two islands are filled with people attending Sunday services. During the week it is not uncommon for other services, such as Bible readings and seminars, to be offered.

Today, almost half of the population belongs to the Anglican Church, which is quite remarkable given its history in Antigua and Barbuda. Before the abolition of slavery, the Anglican Church helped plantation owners, doing little to teach the slaves to read and write. In fact, slaves were often refused entry into church premises.

Left: **A church made of the distinctive green lime-stone from quarries of Antigua and Barbuda.**

Opposite: **Worshippers of various Christian denominations and other religions enjoy religious freedom in Antigua and Barbuda.**

Music is such an important part of Antiguan and Barbudan society that even the ever-present steel band can be found in churches during Sunday service.

THE ANGLICAN COMMUNION

The name of the Anglican Church in Antigua and Barbuda is the Church in the Province of the West Indies. This church was established as self-governing in 1883 and consists of two mainland dioceses, or districts, under a bishop's control, and six island dioceses. Antigua and Barbuda belongs to the diocese of the North Eastern Caribbean and Aruba, which consists of 12 islands.

Those who worship in the Anglican Church consider themselves to be followers of Jesus Christ. The church asserts that its origins come from Christ and His apostles. Because the church is governed by bishops, it is also known as an Episcopal church.

The Anglican Communion is a worldwide association of all Anglican churches. It recognizes the Church of England as the original church. The religious head of the Church of England is the archbishop of Canterbury.

Even though he has no power or authority outside of England, he is still considered a symbolic head for all Anglican churches.

Each church is run autonomously. However, any rites performed by one Anglican church are recognized by the others. Each church has the freedom to determine its own doctrine and religious ceremonies, and its own legislative rules, overseen by a local bishop. The bishop responsible for the diocese of the North Eastern Caribbean and Aruba lives in Saint John's, Antigua. Membership numbers for this diocese is about 60,000.

MORAVIANS

The Moravians were the first to do missionary work among the slaves. During the 18th century they worked hard to establish churches throughout the West Indies, such as Saint Thomas, Saint Croix, and Antigua.

The Moravian's origins are based in ancient Bohemia and Moravia, which are now provinces of the Czech Republic. The churches' precepts began by a rebel Christian preacher named John Huss. He studied theology at the University of Prague and was appointed as a priest around 1400. While studying theology Huss read the writings of John Wyclif, an English religious reformer. Even though Wyclif's writings were condemned by the University of Prague, Huss translated them into the Czech language.

As time passed Huss developed many disagreements with the Roman Catholic church and its practices. During his sermons, he attacked abuses of the Catholic church to his congregation. He was excommunicated from the church and forced into exile. At this time he wrote many manuscripts

A Moravian church in the village of Liberta, one of the first "free" villages to appear in Antigua and Barbuda after the abolition of slavery.

that were influenced by Wyclif's writings. He also refused to acknowledge the absolute power of the pope. He felt that scripture should be the ruling law of any church. He was eventually accused of heresy by the Catholic church and burned at the stake in 1415.

After his death his followers established the Moravian Church in 1457. Up until 1722 most Moravians came from Bohemia and Moravia. After that time the churches' teachings began to spread throughout the world. The Moravian religion is considered to be one of the first Protestant religions of the world.

A Moravian missionary, Samuel Isles, first arrived in Antigua in 1756. His purpose was to preach to the slaves. In Saint John's the slaves would

Saint John's Cathedral is one of the most famous landmarks in Antigua and Barbuda.

sit with a Moravian teacher under a Sandbox tree on Sunday to begin their Sunday school lesson, which not only included Bible precepts, but also how to read and write. Moravian churches soon sprang up throughout the island, and by 1823, schools were attached to these churches. By the time the slaves were freed, over half of them were converted Moravians.

METHODISTS

Methodism was also popular. One of its first missionaries was Nathanial Gilbert. He was born in Antigua in 1721 and was the son to a slave and plantation owner. When Gilbert got older, he went to England to study law. When he returned to Antigua, he entered the House of Assembly.

Gilbert returned to England in 1758 after a spate of illness. There, he was converted by John Wesley, an early leader in the Methodist movement. In 1759 Gilbert returned to Antigua and began preaching Methodism to the slaves. Other missionaries soon followed. They taught the slaves about the spiritual equality of all people and urged them to obey their masters. Methodists also set up schools in various areas of the island. Today, the Moravian and Methodist churches are still well attended in Antigua.

OTHER CHRISTIAN RELIGIONS

About 10 percent of all Antiguans and Barbudans belong to the Roman Catholic church. The bishop for the diocese of Saint John's Basseterre also lives in Saint John's.

Other Christian religious groups include Lutherans, Seventh Day Adventists, Latter Day Saints, and Pentecostals. Baptist churches are upbeat on Sunday mornings, when loud clapping and singing can be heard.

Opposite: **Followers of Rastafarism believe that the coronation of Haile Selassie in 1930 was the fulfilment of Marcus Mosiah Garvey's prophecy.**

THE ANTIGUAN CHRISTIAN COUNCIL

The Anglican, Methodist, Moravian, and Roman Catholic churches and the Salvation Army all joined together to form the Antigua Christian Council. The purpose of this council is to promote understanding and respect between different Christian groups.

Encouraging peace during politically unstable and troubled times is a very important aspect of this council. Prior to the 2004 election, the council created a code of ethics that promoted fair play and denounced any violence during demonstrations or between groups. Each candidate in the election signed and agreed to the code of ethics.

RASTAFARIANISM

Even though the Rastafarian hairstyle of dreadlocks is very common, there are no more than 1,500 Antiguans and Barbudans who actively practice Rastafarianism. This religion gets its inspiration from a variety of sources. Followers read the Old Testament and the book of Revelation in the Bible. The majority of the Bible is rejected by Rastafarians, who believe that its original context was altered by Babylon, also thought of as the white power. Instead, Rastafarians use the Holy Piby, also called the Black Man's Bible. In addition, they place special significance on an Ethiopian Holy Book called the Kebra Negast.

The Ethiopian emperor, Haile Selassie, who lived from 1892 to 1975, is considered a religious symbol for God incarnated by the Rastafarians. Selassie, however, was not a Rastafarian. Instead, he was a follower of the Ethiopian Orthodox Christian Church his entire life.

The Rastafarian religion began with Marcus Mosiah Garvey (1887–1940), a Jamaican who encouraged black people to return to Africa, their rightful homeland. Garvey wanted the dignity of black people restored to Africa. He told his followers that Africa would crown a great king. When that happened they would know that deliverance was upon them. The coronation of Selassie in 1930 was considered to be the fulfillment of Garvey's prophecy.

OTHER FAITHS

Buddhism is another religion that has a small but dedicated following in Antigua and Barbuda. Regular meetings are set up where members can discuss their faith or chant.

The Baha'i Faith has a base in Saint John's. This religion believes that all humanity is a single race and that one day total global unification will be a reality. Its followers believe that God has set up various events to break down barriers between races, classes, and nations. Once these events are complete, a world civilization will arise. Currently, there are about 50 members of the Baha'i Faith.

Another religion practiced in Antigua and Barbuda is Islam. However, it has a very small following.

THE STATE FLAG of ANTIGUA & BARBUDA

The Golden sun symbolises The dawn of a new era.
Red symbolises The dynamism of The people.
Blue symbolises hope.
Black symbolises The soil and our African heritage.
Gold, Blue and **White** Together represent Antigua's Tourist attractions — sun, sea, sand.
The "V" depicted in The design by The Black, Blue, and White band is The symbol of victory.

GOD BLESS OUR NATION

1775 B.C. FIRST RECORDED DATE OF MAN IN ANTIGUA AND BARBUDA
C. 35 A.D. ARAWAKS FROM SOUTH AMERICA SETTLED IN ANTIGUA AND BARBUDA
1493 COLUMBUS NAMED ANTIGUA AFTER CATHEDRAL IN SEVILLE, SPAIN
1632 ENGLISH COLONISED ANTIGUA UNDER EDWARD WARNER
1640s SUGAR AND SLAVERY INTRODUCED
1666 THE FRENCH HELD ANTIGUA FOR THREE MONTHS
1736 PRINCE KLAAS PLOTTED A SLAVE INSURRECTION
1808 END OF SLAVE TRADE
1834 EMANCIPATION OF THE SLAVES
1939 THE TRADE UNION ERA BEGAN
1967 INDEPENDENCE IN ASSOCIATION WITH GREAT BRITAIN
1981 FULL INDEPENDENCE

LANGUAGE

THE OFFICIAL LANGUAGE OF ANTIGUA and Barbuda is English, but the majority of people speak Antiguan Creole, which is a mix of English, local slang, and West African expressions. Antiguan Creole developed during British rule as a way for plantation owners and slaves to communicate with each other—hence, it is a hybrid or mix of their languages.

Antigua and Barbuda is a predominantly bilingual society and the two languages that are most commonly used are English and Antiguan Creole. Standard English is the language used in schools and by the government, and Antiguan Creole is used in everyday speech. Most Antiguans and Barbudans speak Antiguan Creole and can switch from English to Creole quite easily.

ANTIGUAN CREOLE

Linguists, or specialists in the science of languages who have studied Antiguan Creole have found very definite West African words in the language, but the majority of changes involve English words that are shaped into Creole words; for example, *give* becomes *gee* in Antiguan Creole. Such Creole words came about because African languages do not have a sound for *v* or *th*. This made it difficult for slaves to pronounce words with these sounds. Words were changed to omit these sounds: *think* is pronounced as *tink, live* is said as *lib*.

English grammar usages are also altered in Antiguan Creole. For example, "He is my father" might become "him my father," which omits the verb *is* and uses an objective pronoun as the subject. Possessive pronouns are sometimes replaced by an objective pronoun, for instance, "You walk to my house" might be changed to "you walk me house." Not only is the pronoun changed, but the preposition *to* is also left out.

Opposite: **A poster in English explaining the elements of the flag of Antigua and Barbuda.**

There are also many West African expressions that are in Antiguan Creole. *Bassa bassa* means fooling around. *Catta* is a cloth that is placed on the head to help in carrying a large or heavy load. A man who is easily manipulated by a woman is called a *kunumunu*. These are just a few of the West African expressions that have found their way into the language.

MASS MEDIA

The government-owned Antigua and Barbuda Broadcasting Service provides radio and television to the two islands. Some other broadcasts are Observer Radio, Radio ZDK, Caribbean Radio Lighthouse, and CTV

LOCAL ANTIGUAN PHRASES

"Me na know wey dat dey!" means "I don't know where it is!"
"Smady" means "somebody"
"Breeze off" means "take a rest"
"Down wet-up" means "throw water at"
"Wagy" means "clothes"
"Wey you a go?" means "where are you going?
"Na badda me" means "don't bother me"
"She garn a choch" means "she has gone to church"
"Wey de food garn!" means "where has the food gone!"
"Me na min no" means "I do not know"
"Sen de money giee me" means "send me the money"
"Me nar tek um" means "I am not taking it"
"You dif?" means "are you deaf?"
"E bark worse dan e bite" means "he talks more than he acts"
"Whey it drop it tap" means "I will use up what I have now"

Entertainment Systems, which provides 33 U.S. channels 24 hours a day. The majority of households in the country own a TV and radio.

Barbuda has a homemade-type radio station called MRS radio station. To set this up, a local man, Ordrick Samuel, bolted two loud speakers on either end of his home. He begins his program at 6:00 in the morning. He lets people know about upcoming events, talks about the history of Barbuda, sometimes has an evangelist speak, or airs a program on marriage. MRS radio station is financed by businesses buying advertising time.

The *Antigua Sun* and the *Daily Observer* are the two major newspapers in the country. These papers are published throughout the week, except for Sundays. Smaller publications are the *Outlet, National Informer,* and the *Worker's Voice.*

PUBLIC LIBRARY

Antigua has a small public library. It is on a floor above a fabric store in Saint John's. The library is not computerized, which means the cataloging and checking out of books is kept track of by hand. The government has been allocating money to build a large library, but to date it has not been completed.

Barbuda currently does not have a public library. But the Barbuda Library Association has been trying to raise funds to build a library for several years. Drawings have been made for the new library building. In addition, a lot of land has been fenced and cleared, ready for construction. Insufficient funding is the only reason the library has not been built.

Samuel Ordrick is a well-known radio personality in Antigua and Barbuda.

ARTS

ART FOUND IN ANTIGUA AND Barbuda is varied. But, no matter what it is, from music to storytelling to pottery, it all has a West Indies influence. Many artists call Antigua their home. Some came from overseas and others from poor villages in Antigua. Some forms of art have changed dramatically or did not exist in the early days, whereas others have stayed almost the same since the days of slavery.

MUSIC HISTORY

During the slave period English and African music merged. The result of this combination in Antigua and Barbuda was a type of music called *bennah*. This music is similar to other African-Caribbean music in that it is a litany or telling of facts and details. The themes of these songs were ones of praise, or ridicule, or women. The singers made up the words to the songs as they went along and were often accompanied by drums. These types of songs brought mental and emotional relief to the African slaves working in the fields and gave them a means to express their ideas and opinions.

One of the most famous *bennah* singers lived in the middle of the twentieth century. His name was John Quarkoo. He was known for making public announcements, relaying the latest gossip, or singing about up-to-date topics, always with satire and wit. He ridiculed the oppressors of the black Antiguans and even found himself in jail with the charge of slander. This talented *bennah* singer made up his lyrics on the spot.

During the 1940s and 1950s, *bennah* was the main nonreligious music in Antigua and Barbuda. It was later replaced by Trinidad Calypso, which has strong rhythms with energetic ballads that deal with current affairs through satire. Because of the historical importance of *bennah,* it is still played today at cultural events.

Opposite: **Local paintings on display on the streets of Antigua and Barbuda.**

Steel bands are a fixture at most celebrations and festivals.

MUSIC TODAY

Music is very important to Antiguan and Barbudans and can be heard everywhere. A wide variety of music exists, including reggae, jazz, hip-hop, gospel, steel pan, and calypso. Among the wide variety of music that can be heard in Antigua and Barbuda, West Indian rhythms are the most predominant.

The most popular music is calypso because it is easy to dance to and is very entertaining. Calypso lyrics may address controversial subjects of the day or local gossip. Through this type of music, calypso artists can freely comment on local political situations or social problems. Not only are calypso artists singers, they are also actors who use dramatic gestures to entertain.

During Carnival, the most celebrated and colorful festival in Antigua, calypso singers compete fiercely against one another during the calypso competition. While performing in their tents, they use any

THE HISTORY OF FOLK SONGS

During the days of slavery, Africans were not allowed to talk to each other while working on the plantation. To communicate or talk about the hard times they had to endure, folk songs were created. These songs were not written by a single person. Instead, a group of people would create the songs, which talked about social or economic situations. As time passed and slavery became a thing of the past, the folk songs in Antigua became more upbeat and happy.

Hard Work
We work till Jesus come
We work
Like son of man
We work
Till Jesus come
We work
A fork de land
We work
A cut de cane
We work
A dig de root
We work
A hold de bakkra plough
We work
A work till Jesus come
We work
A work like son of man
We work
We work till Jesus come
We work

Beautiful Antigua
Antigua, so beautiful; Antigua, so wonderful
Beaches plentiful, climate healthy
People peaceable, life so lengthy
Hospitality full and plenty
Antigua

method possible to get people to come inside. Large audiences not only demonstrate popularity, but it also helps with CD sales. The top 10 or 12 singers compete against each other in front of thousands of fans. Once the top calypso artist is named, he or she is titled Monarch of the Antigua Calypso Competition.

Calypso singers are considered to be celebrities in Antigua and Barbuda. Their records are played on the radio and articles are printed about them in the local paper.

Reggae is also popular. This type of music originated in Jamaica in the 1960s. It is often thought to be part of the Rastafarian movement, but reggae music covers other topics besides politics, such as love. There are many groups in Antigua that play reggae music. It can be heard at local restaurants, as well as major concerts.

Steel pans or drums are very common. Steel bands began to appear in almost every village and town in Antigua and Barbuda by the middle of the 1900s. Today, steel bands can be heard playing at Shirley Heights for the weekly six-hour party held every Sunday. Steel band music fills the air during the barbecue and people dance and drink while vendors sell handmade jewelry and baskets. Steel bands can also be heard at major

NATIONAL MUSIC OF ANTIGUA

Music made by a fife band is part of Antigua's history. A fife is a small flute that is often cut from a piece of bamboo. On its top are six to eight holes. This instrument was usually homemade, so it was easy for poor Antiguans from olden times to own one.

Other instruments found in a fife band are a grater, a large piece of pipe blown on one end called a Boom pipe, a ukulele, and guitars. Currently, the best known fife band in Antigua and Barbuda is called the Rio Band, which is made up of five or six players.

THE MOODS OF PAN

In 1999 the Gemonites Steel Orchestra organized an annual steel band festival in Antigua called the Moods of Pan. Today, bands come from all over the world to compete, including Canada, France, the United States, Grenada, and Trinidad.

This festival began as a single concert in November 1999. Because of the overwhelming response from the Antiguan public, the Moods of Pan became a three-day festival in 2000. That year the festival featured famous steel bands. It also began the largest steel band competition in the world, called "Keep Pan Alive with Five," which is now called "Five-Alive." To compete, five members perform a five-minute arrangement of music. The music is based on the artist or group that has been selected to be honored that year. Each band can score a total of 100 points. Scoring is based on music quality, performance, and the response of the crowd. Today, the Moods of Pan has been expanded to run over four days and is sponsored by the Ministry of Tourism.

THE MUSEUM OF ANTIGUA AND BARBUDA

Located in Saint John's old courthouse, the Museum of Antigua and Barbuda is devoted to safeguarding its history. It was opened in 1985 and is run by the Historical and Archaeological Society. Its exhibit tells the story of Antigua and Barbuda's natural, social, and political history. Throughout the years it has collected many historical objects and has compiled a vast database of information.

The museum also has an educational program. Lectures are given to schoolchildren about history and it also organizes field trips to visit historical sites. In addition, it organizes cultural evenings for the general public.

hotels, festivals, and at Carnival. Some famous steel bands in Antigua are the Harmonites, Halcyon, and the Gemonites.

Traditional music played by orchestras and brass bands can also be found in Antigua. One of the best bands for this type of music is the Laviscount Brass, which has played at government functions.

PRISCILLA LOOBY'S ART STUDIO

This local artist's studio can be found along the road leading to English Harbor. Looby was born and raised in Liberta, a small village. She began sketching when she was a little girl. In 1982 a peace corps volunteer came to Antigua and taught Looby how to use acrylic paints. Since that time she has painted many pictures from the images she remembers as a young child. Her brightly colored paintings are of village scenes and have been sold to visitors from all over the world.

ANTIGUAN WRITERS

The theme of most Antiguan writers is island life. Jamaica Kincaid is probably the most famous author who was born in Antigua. She has written novels, short stories, and essays about her life in Antigua. A couple of her novels are *A Small Place* and *Annie John.*

She was born in 1949 with the name Elaine Potter Richardson. She lived with her mother and stepfather until she left Antigua in 1965 to live in New York State. She completed her secondary education there and continued her education at Franconia College in New Hampshire. Because her parents did not approve of her writing, she changed her name to Jamaica Kincaid in 1973. She worked as a staff writer for the *New Yorker* for many years. Today, she is married and has two children.

A more recent Antiguan writer is Joanne C. Hillhouse, who also writes under a pen name—Jhohadli. Her books include *The Boy from Willow Bend, On Becoming,* and *Dancing Nude in the Moonlight,* which was published in 2004 by Macmillan. She also helped produce Antigua and Barbuda's first and second feature films, *The Sweetest Mango* and *No Seed.* Hillhouse has been involved in television production and freelance journalism for local publications. Because of her various contributions to literacy and the literary arts of Antigua and Barbuda, she received a United National Educational Scientific and Cultural Organization (UNESCO) award.

An important part of Antiguan history was preserved by two authors, Keithlyn B. Smith and Fernando C. Smith. They compiled a book titled *To Shoot Hard Labour*. This book is a biography of their grandfather, Mr. Samuel "Papa Sammy" Smith. It is unique in that it has captured the history of Antigua from a black Antiguan's viewpoint. Most history written during the 19th century was written by white Europeans.

POTTERY

Some of the first settlers in Antigua, the Arawaks, brought pottery to and made it in Antigua. Making pottery continued throughout the slave era.

Decorative pieces of pottery on Antigua and Barbuda.

African slaves in Antigua and Barbuda would make pottery out of local clay. This pottery was used for cooking.

Today, there are several potters in Antigua. They make pottery from clay, paper clay, terra-cotta clay, and glass. The materials are formed into bowls, plates, flowerpots, mobiles, and decorative pots. At Seaview Farm Antiguan women make coal pots and cooking pots out of red and white clay that is found locally. Most pottery made today is for decoration.

A native Antiguan, Nancy Nicholson, has been making clay pots using local clay for over 20 years. She is inspired by the beauty of the Caribbean Sea, as well as indigenous artwork. Her pots are famous for their Arawak motifs. She uses fish, the ocean, and lizards in her designs.

ART STUDIOS

Many other types of artists live and work in Antigua. There are graphic designers, sculptors, painters, scrimshaw artists, and photographers, all with a Caribbean theme.

Colorful scenes of Antiguan and Barbudan life are a distinctive feature of locally-produced paintings.

Sculptures are designed into fish and birds. Paintings of seascapes and boats of the Caribbean are made with watercolor, oil, and acrylic. Frogs, dolphins, seahorses, and pineapples are carved into bone by scrimshaw artists. One artist makes hand-painted pictures of Antigua and Barbuda. Throughout Antigua are several art galleries displaying the talents of its local artists.

LEISURE

THE LEISURE PURSUITS OF ANTIGUA and Barbuda are a combination of games and sports that have been taken from its African roots and its long affiliation with England. Also, because it is surrounded by the Caribbean Sea, a variety of water sports and activities have become common.

THE GAME OF WARRI

Antigua and Barbuda's national board game is *warri* meaning "house." *Warri* is a thinking game like chess and backgammon. It was brought to the West Indies by slaves from West Africa during the sugar era.

The *warri* game board is a rectangular wooden board that is sometimes very ornately carved. It has 12 hollows, or houses, designed with six on each side. At each end of the board are larger houses for capturing the *nickars,* which are small nuts found in the Antiguan bush.

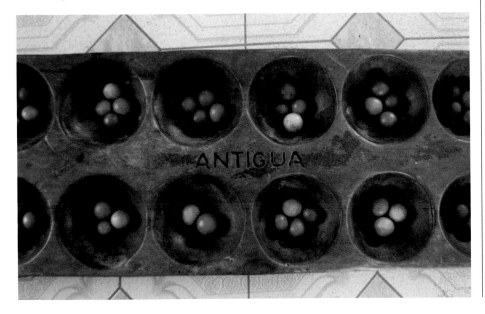

Left: **The game of *warri* is immensely popular among Antiguans and Barbudans.**

Opposite: **Cricket is a popular sport enjoyed on Antigua and Barbuda.**

NICKARS

The marble size *nickars* come from the spiky seedpods of the Nickar tree. When these pods open the seeds fall out. There are brown, gray, and white seeds. In the past the white *nickar* seeds were ground up and made into local coffee.

It is played by two opponents. They both start with 24 counters, or *nickars*. The players place 4 *nickars* in each of their 6 houses on the board, making the total *nickars* on the board 48. To win one player must capture 25 *nickars*. This is accomplished by a variety of techniques, such as a quick ability to calculate, verbal pressure, and skillful movements.

Warri has become part of the Mind Sports Olympiad, which is a festival featuring more than 40 different thinking games. The Mind Sports Olympiad organization is based in London, England. In Antigua the National Warri Festival is held in October. During the festival the best players are determined with an overall champion. *Warri* is also played throughout the year at various rum shops in Antigua.

A CHILD'S GAME

The children of Antigua and Barbuda have many games, some of which involve singing. *Ponchinella* is one of those games. To play the game children must form a circle with one child in the middle. The children start clapping and singing:

Look who's here Ponchinella, Ponchinella
Look who's here Ponchinella, Ponchinella
Look who's here Ponchinella in the shoe
(Here they point to the child in the middle, and the other kids continue singing.)

What can you do Ponchinella, Ponchinella
What can you do Ponchinella, Ponchinella
What can you do Ponchinella in the shoe
(The child in the center makes a face or does a dance, and the other kids continue singing while copying the child in the center.)

We can do it too Ponchinella, Ponchinella
We can do it too Ponchinella, Ponchinella
(The child in the center then starts to spin around with his or her finger pointed, and the other kids continue singing.)

Who's coming next Ponchinella, Ponchinella
Who's coming next Ponchinella, Ponchinella
Who's coming next Ponchinella in the shoe
(The child in the center stops, and the other kids sing. . .)

That's You!
(The child being pointed at must now enter the middle of the circle, and the song starts over again.)

DOMINOES

Another popular pastime game is dominoes. This game is played in nearly all the villages around Antigua and Barbuda and is an international game. Recently, Trevor Simon won the Antiguan championship and represented Antigua in the domino tournament held in England. There are many variations to this game, but the most common version uses 28 domino pieces. The domino pieces are placed facedown on the table and then shuffled around by the players. There are usually two players and each selects seven dominoes. One player starts by placing a domino on the table face up. The opponent player must lay a domino with the same value next to the first domino with the like value sides touching. Then, the other player must do the same, and so on. The winner is the first person to run out of dominoes.

SPORTS

Antiguans and Barbudans participate in a variety of sports, including basketball, volleyball, golf, tennis, and horseback racing, which is done in Barbuda every two weeks. Other sports are car racing, scuba diving, snorkeling, jet skiing, waterskiing, fishing, and soccer, which is sometimes played in a field where goats are grazing on the hillsides. But none of these are as popular as cricket and sailing.

CRICKET

Cricket fans in Antigua and Barbuda are fiercely devoted and often pack the stadiums during cricket matches. International matches are televised so everyone can watch the games. Cricket season begins in Antigua during the month of January and lasts through July. But this sport is wildly popular on the twin-island country and is played at every opportunity throughout the year. To ensure the preservation of cricket Antigua and Barbuda, the Antigua Cricket Association was formed.

HOW CRICKET IS PLAYED This game started during the Dark Ages as a simple game of batting an object, such as a piece of wood, between

ANTIGUAN CRICKET CHAMPIONS

Four of the West Indies' best cricket players over the last 30 years have been Antiguans. They are Andy Roberts, Richie Richardson, Curtley Ambrose, and one of the greatest cricket players of all time, Sir Vivian Richards.

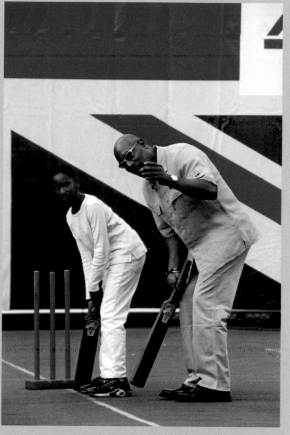

Andy Roberts played during the mid-1970s. He became known as an extremely fast bowler. Richie Richardson was known as one of the most talented and aggressive batsmen in the 1980s. Curtley Ambrose began playing cricket in 1988. He was an intensely fast bowler. Because of his competitive reputation, top batsmen feared playing against Curtley Ambrose.

Sir Vivian Richards (*right*) began playing cricket professionally in 1974. In 1975 the first international match for the Cricket World Cup was held in England. The teams playing were England, Australia, New Zealand, the West Indies, India, Pakistan, Sri Lanka, and East Africa. The final match was between Australia and the West Indies. The West Indies team beat Australia by 17 runs. Richards was part of this team. In 1979 the next Cricket World Cup was held. Richards was named Man of the Match. During this competition he led the West Indies team to victory against England by scoring 138 runs. In total the West Indies team beat England by 92 runs. Sir Vivian Richards is still revered in Antigua today. The Museum of Antigua and Barbuda is home to Richards' cricket bat. Because of his outstanding record, he received an honorary knighthood and was named one of the top five cricketers in the world.

two players. The game evolved into having 11 players on each team. A cricket ball and bat are used during the game. A cricket ball weighs more but is a little bit smaller than a baseball. The cricket bat is wooden and measures 38 inches (96.5 cm) long by 4.25 inches (10.8 cm) wide. The bat has a handle and a flat wooden paddle called a blade.

Cricket can be played on a grassy field or in a stadium. The central rectangular area is called a pitch and is 22 yards (20 m) long. Two standing wickets are placed at either end of the pitch. The wickets consist of three vertical sticks that are 2.5 feet high (75 cm) and called stumps, with two small horizontal pieces called bails resting on top of them.

Each team has a chance to bat. When one team is up to bat, the other team is in the field, except for a bowler, whose role is similar to the pitcher in baseball. Two batsmen are up at one time. They are positioned on opposite ends of the pitch. One of the batsmen is up to bat, or "on strike," while another waits to make a run. The bowler pitches the ball at the batting batsman. The bowler tries to aim the ball at the bails to knock them off or to strike the batter out. If the batsman hits the ball hard enough, he and the waiting batsmen can make a run. The batting team scores when both batsmen run to their opposite wickets. The winning team is the one with the highest number of runs.

Antigua has several cricket fields, such as the Antigua Recreation Ground and the Stanford Cricket Ground. But the top cricket stadium currently under construction is the Sir Vivian Richards Cricket Stadium, which is located 4 miles (6.5 km) east of Saint John's. This stadium is being built by the Chinese government in coordination with the Antiguan government for the 2007 Cricket World Cup.

Cricket, which was introduced to Antigua and Barbuda by the British, is immensely popular in the West Indies.

GIRLS' SOFTBALL CRICKET

Cricket is not only popular with men, but with women, too. Antigua and Barbuda has a national women's cricket team. The players range from age 15 to 50 years old.

Women's cricket is played with a softball that is lighter than in men's cricket and also easier to pitch. There are about 40 women's teams throughout the country. Almost each village has a men's and a women's team. Each woman's team decides on a name. One team's name was "Strictly Business." The teams have sponsors that buy their uniforms and equipment. If the team has to travel to another island to play, they will conduct fundraisers to make money.

During the month of April and May, scouts will watch the various women's teams play to find the best players. These players are then asked to join the national team. Once the national team is formed, it will play the other islands for the championship title. The best team in all the islands is announced in the multipurpose facility in Saint John's. It is then presented with a trophy and money.

Sailing is a major pasttime in Antigua and Barbuda.

SAILING

Because Antigua and Barbuda are surrounded by water and has continuous trade winds, sailing is very popular. In the past sailing was the only means of traveling long distances across water. Today, sailing is considered a sport.

Because of the popularity of sailing, there are two yacht clubs in Antigua: the Antigua Yacht Club and the Jolly Harbor Yacht Club. In addition, Nicholson's Charter Yacht Show is held once a year before Christmas.

FESTIVALS

ANTIGUA AND BARBUDA HAS 10 national holidays. The Christian national holidays are Good Friday, Easter Monday, Whit Monday, and Christmas. The rest of the holidays are nonreligious. These are New Year's Day, Labor Day, the Queen's Official Birthday, Vere Cornwall Bird Sr. Day, Carnival, and Independence Day. New Year's Eve is also celebrated throughout Antigua, but is known as Old Year's Night.

In addition to public holidays, there are many local and national festivals that take place during the year, such as the Antigua International Hot Air Balloon Festival, Antigua Sun Annual Kite Flying Competition, Classic Yacht Regatta, Antigua Sailing Week, Heritage Day, and Wadadli Day, a festival that was added in 1997. Wadadli Day was created to celebrate everything Antiguan, including the national costume. It is held in the Botanical Gardens in Saint John's. All food, dress, and entertainment at this celebration is indigenous to Antigua.

Above: **A girl playing steel drums. Music is an integral part of any festival on Antigua and Barbuda.**

Opposite: **A local woman dressed in traditional clothing at one of Antigua and Barbuda's many festivals.**

CARNIVAL

This festival celebrates the emancipation of the slaves and lasts for about 10 days. All Antiguans, young and old, celebrate from July through to the beginning of August. Celebrators wear costumes made from a rainbow of colors, such as pink, purple, green, red, turquoise, orange, blue, silver, and gold. During the festival talent shows are held, as well as a parade of bands. There are several beauty pageants, and the biggest honor of all is to be crowned the Carnival Queen. Once crowned, the Carnival Queen reigns for one year. During this time she is a traveling ambassador for Antigua.

Calypso music is an important part of Carnival. During the festivals, calypso competitions are some of the main events. The last competition in Carnival determines who will wear the Calypso Monarch's crown. The winner is crowned late on Sunday night or sometimes very early Monday morning.

The French word, *j'ouvert,* describes the climax of the Carnival celebration. The word translates roughly to mean, "This is your last chance to celebrate, so live it up!" The *j'ouvert* begins on the first Monday in August at 4:00 A.M. when Antiguans swarm into the streets. Everybody begins to dance along the streets of Saint John's. Decorative floats and

Brightly colored costumes and props are a common feature in the boisterous, noisy Carnival celebrations.

bands make their way through the crowds. The final street dancing is on Tuesday, from dusk to midnight, when Carnival is officially over. The next day Antigua is extremely quiet and peaceful while everyone recovers from the festivities.

Barbuda holds its own Carnival in May or June called Caribana. Even though it is shorter than the one on Antigua, it has a talented teen competition, a beach bash, and horse racing. Local Barbudans say that Carnival on its island is not to celebrate emancipation, but rather just to celebrate life.

THE HISTORY OF CHRISTMAS IN ANTIGUA

Antiguans have always loved the Christmas season. In the past the Christmas season began about three weeks before Christmas Day. It started with carol singers carrying a carol tree throughout Saint John's. A carol tree was constructed of wood with crossbars that acted as arms for hanging Japanese lanterns.

The week before Christmas saw the most activity, with masqueraders walking the streets and music being played everywhere. Acrobats and tumblers performed dressed in colorful and sometimes silly costumes. At home, women made a new dress for each of the three days of Christmas. This was a time when everyone was dressed in their Sunday best.

Other past Christmas traditions were long ghosts and John Bulls. Long ghosts were 12 feet (3.6 m) high. A mask was cut in the top section for the eyes, nose, and frightening-looking teeth. These masqueraders roamed the streets to get donations for Christmas.

John Bull originated as a political cartoon. It was a character who was supposed to represent England in a funny way. Men who dressed up as John Bull in Antigua and Barbuda wore ugly masks similar to those of African witch doctors. Their heads were topped with bull horns. The intent was to look as grotesque as possible. John Bulls would terrorize and excite anyone around them. A cattle tender or another person next to a John Bull carried a whip. He would crack it over the John Bull's head, making the John Bull run toward the screaming audience. Even though John Bulls no longer come out during the Christmas season, they can sometimes still be seen during Carnival festivities or during a jump up in the villages when there is a long weekend holiday.

CHRISTMAS TODAY

Christmas season in Antigua begins in late November when all the radio stations begin to play Christmas songs. Christmas bazaars selling arts and crafts are set up at schools and churches. The streets of Saint John's are adorned with Christmas decorations. Homes are also decorated with Christmas trees and lights. Christmas programs, pageants, and carol services are held at schools and churches reciting, acting, and singing about the story of Christmas.

Souse, or headcheese, is often eaten on Christmas Eve. This cheese is more like a jellied loaf. It is called headcheese because it is made from the meaty parts from the head of a pig. The pig's trotters are also included. The headcheese is prepared by simmering the head until the meat falls off and the liquid becomes a jellylike broth. The meat is chopped, seasoned, and then put back in the broth which is then placed in a mold and chilled until it is firm.

A local drink prepared only during Christmas is called sorrel. It comes from the sorrel herb, which grows flowers with red petals. These petals are removed and put into a glass jar with cinnamon, hot water, and a few grains of rice. This mixture could be left for days or weeks. If it is left for days, it makes a nice drink. If it is left for weeks, it makes a pleasant-tasting wine.

Breakfast on Christmas is usually ham, eggs, and bread. Baking the Christmas dinner is an important part of the day. Food such as roasted turkey, ham, or a beef roast, candied sweet potatoes, peas and rice, salad, and Christmas cake and pudding might be prepared for the Christmas feast. An adopted Portuguese dish that may be served is *vinadarlush*. This dish is made of pork that is marinated in fresh herbs and apple cider, which is then either fried or served with gravy.

Barbuda has its own traditions during the Christmas season. Celebrations on this island usually involve all local residents. To start the Christmas season on December 15, one local resident has a porridge party. During the party a variety of different porridges are served, such as cornmeal, rice, oats, and cream of wheat. Everyone comes and helps themselves to as much porridge as they can eat.

Sometimes, on Christmas Eve, December 24, a fundraising drive is organized. The drive is fun and lively, more like a party with food for sale and local entertainment.

On Old Year's Night, December 31, a Bush Tea party is planned that starts at around 8:00 P.M. A variety of teas are served. Some are made from local plants found in the bush. Food such as ham rolls, sausage, and cheese is also provided.

ANTIGUA CLASSIC YACHT REGATTA

Half of the entire month of April is dedicated to sailing. The Antigua Classic Yacht Regatta kicks off in the middle of the month. The purpose of this regatta, or race, is to unite owners and crew members of classic and traditional yachts. Racing enthusiasts come from all over the world to participate.

Yachts joining this race must follow certain guidelines. The yacht itself must be a true classic. These graceful sailing ships were commonly built years ago. They are distinguished by their large fluttering sails and smoothly built hulls. To be considered a true classic, each yacht entry must have a full keel made of wood or steel. In addition, its rig and look have to be traditional.

The regatta's courses are set up so that these older vessels can sail easily no matter what their size. The emphasis in this race is not on winning, but rather on sailing together with other classics and enjoying the Caribbean Sea.

ANTIGUA SAILING WEEK

The end of April and beginning of May is Antigua Sailing Week, which takes place over five days. Over 5,000 people come to watch about 1,500 people on 200 yachts race on some of the biggest and fastest sailing yachts in the world. Twenty-four countries in 2005 were represented

in the race. It is known as the largest regatta in the Caribbean, as well as one of the top three regattas in the world. It is sponsored by the Antigua Hotels and Tourist Association.

Billowing white sails blow in the wind as the sail boats creak and sway in the blue waters of the Caribbean. Races such as Dickenson Bay Race, Jolly Harbor Race, Ocean Race, and Bareboat Challenge are held. Trophies are awarded to the winners of these races. Top-class judges with backgrounds at Olympic regattas and world championships monitor the events.

In addition, every year for sailing week there is a poster competition held for children ages 5 to 16. The theme of the posters is anything that represents sailing and the English Harbor. The winner's poster is displayed in English Harbor during sailing week. In 2005 a 16-year-old won the contest.

Rivalry is intense in the numerous sailing competitions that are held in Antigua and Barbuda.

FOOD

EUROPEAN DISHES ARE FOUND throughout Antigua. French and Italian restaurants are open throughout Saint John's. English dishes such as fish and chips are also served. But Antigua has its own local specialties that have a Caribbean flair. Though the dishes are not hot and spicy, hot pepper sauce can be found on almost every table within Antigua.

ANTIGUAN SPICES

Herbs and spices are grown in gardens throughout the country. They are used to flavor dishes, as well as to attempt to cure the sick. Some common herbs and spices used are rosemary, thyme, basil, and allspice.

Ginger is made into a noncarbonated drink called ginger beer. The outside of the ginger root is scraped and then grated. It is then soaked in water and sugar. This is then pushed through a muslin cloth to make ginger beer.

ANTIGUAN DISHES

One favorite dish in Antigua is called *ducana*. This sweet and salty dish is made of cornmeal, sugar, spices, grated sweet potato, coconut, and pumpkin puree. This combination is mixed up and placed in *ducana* leaves, where it is steamed.

Goat water is considered a specialty dish in Antigua. This poorly named dish is really a delicious spicy stew that is seasoned with cinnamon, cloves, and hot peppers. Goat water is sold throughout Antigua. It can be found in expensive restaurants, as well as at roadside stands.

Above: **A variety of peppers are often used in local dishes.**

Opposite: **Vegetables and fruits are sold in outdoor markets.**

ANTIGUA'S OWN HOT SAUCE

Susie's Hot Sauce was started by local Antiguan Susanna Tonge. Prior to making the sauce, she ran a boardinghouse in Saint John's. During this time she cooked breakfast, lunch, and dinner for her guests. Included in these meals were homemade breads, cakes, and juices. She began experimenting with various combinations of peppers to create her own hot sauce. Tonge dreamed of coming up with a tasty recipe that she could bottle and sell locally. Eventually she came upon a winning combination and created her own brand of hot sauce in the 1960s. She gave her hot sauce the name Susie's Hot Sauce. Even though Tonge has passed away, the business continued through her daughter, Rosie.

In the beginning Tonge cooked the sauce in her backyard using a coal pot. Rosie grew up helping her mother make the hot sauce by grinding the peppers and fanning the coals. Rosie has since made additional hot sauces, such as "Mango Mandingo," "Pineapple Pleasure," and "Tear Drops," which is so hot it brings tears to your eyes. Each of Rosie's sauces are mixed and bottled in her kitchen at her home. Her garage has huge bags of small red chilies, yellow chilies, and green chilies.

Throughout Antigua, Susie's Hot Sauce can be found on almost every table in local restaurants. It has also gone on to win several international awards. In 2001 Rosie entered Susie's Hot Sauce along with several of Rosie's other hot sauces in the Texas Fiery Food Show in Austin, Texas. Susie's Hot Sauce won first place in the habanero hot sauce category and third place in the Caribbean Hot Sauce category.

RUM

Because of Antigua and Barbuda's sugar plantation history, rum has been made there since the mid-1700s. Rum was very important during the colonial era, especially for medical purposes. Even though Nelson's Dockyard had a medical facility, the main medicine used there was rum.

This alcoholic beverage is made by distilling fermented sugar and water. The sugar, of course, comes from sugarcane and is fermented from either molasses or cane juice.

Molasses is made when brown sugar is produced. Once the sugarcane juice has been boiled and all the crystallized sugar has been removed, a sweet, sticky by-product remains.

Fermented sugar is created by taking cane juice or molasses and mixing it with water. This mixture is then fermented and distilled, which produces alcohol. The alcohol is then placed in oak barrels and aged from 2 to over 30 years.

In the early days rum in Antigua consisted of different homemade brews. But the mass produced Cavalier rums began to be made in the 1950s. The first one was called Cavalier Muscovado Rum. Today, a variety of Cavalier rums can still be found throughout the island.

NATIONAL FRUIT

The Antiguan black pineapple is grown mainly on the south side of Antigua. This pineapple is short with a small tipped stem. Its fruit is very sweet and yellow. These pineapples can be bought from roadside vendors who will chop it up in front of you and place it in a plastic bag.

It was brought to Antigua thousands of years ago by the Arawak Indians from South America. It became known as food for the gods.

A colorful display of the fresh fruits and vegetables found at Saint John's market.

FOOD MARKET

The public market in Saint John's, a favorite local food market, is splashed with bright colors from fresh fruits and vegetables, such as yellow lemons, violet eggplants, brown and white onions, bright yellow squash, red chili peppers, and green bananas. It is open daily until 6:00 P.M. It can become especially busy on Fridays and Saturdays.

Across the street is the meat market and fish market. Inside the meat market are refrigeration units filled with large slabs of meat. Butchers stand behind the counter holding huge butcher knives, ready to serve their customers. Some butchers wear nylon hats to hold their long dreadlocks in. Butchers chop the meat on thick chopping blocks.

Outside next to the meat market is the fish market. Piles of fish have hundreds of flies on them. Workers bend over sinks of slimy water next to a chopping block to wash, clean, and chop the fish. The fish is then placed in black plastic bags.

NATIONAL DISH

Fungi and pepperpot is a stew made of yam, pumpkin, peas, okra, eggplant, plantain, dasheen leaves (similar to spinach), squash, and salted meats, topped with fried cornmeal dumplings. This national dish is thought to have originated from the Amerindians long ago living in Antigua. These Indians used to make the stew in a deep clay firepot that was a type of food storage.

TYPICAL MEALS

Meals on Antigua and Barbuda are similar to what is eaten in most Western countries. Breakfast might include cereal, yogurt, or toast with a cup of tea. Lunch might be a sandwich, fried chicken, or soup—basically anything that can be eaten quickly and perhaps bought at the local fast food restaurants or bakeries. Depending on the family's income, some kind of meat will be served at dinnertime, along with a salad or vegetable and rice or pasta.

BREAD PUDDING

¼ cup of butter

2 cups milk

Brown sugar to taste

4–8 slices of bread

¼ teaspoon lemon rind

1 teaspoon vanilla extract

2 eggs, beaten

Dried fruit

Antiguan black pineapple (optional)

Preheat the oven to 275°F (135°C). Spread butter on the bread and then cut the breads into cubes. Place the buttered bread cubes in a bowl. Pour the milk, brown sugar, lemon rind, and vanilla over the bread and gently stir. Add eggs and stir gently. Place half the mixture in a greased pudding dish. Spread with the dried fruit and Antiguan black pineapple, if you desire. Pour the remainder of the mixture in the dish. Place in oven. Bake for 50 minutes or until the pudding is set.

DUCANA

2 large sweet potatoes
½ cup sugar
2½ cups flour
Dash of allspice

Grate sweet potatoes. Add sugar to potatoes and let sit for about an hour. Mix in flour and allspice. Spoon mixture evenly into four to five pieces of foil. Wrap tightly. Place foil wraps into boiling water for 45 minutes until firm.

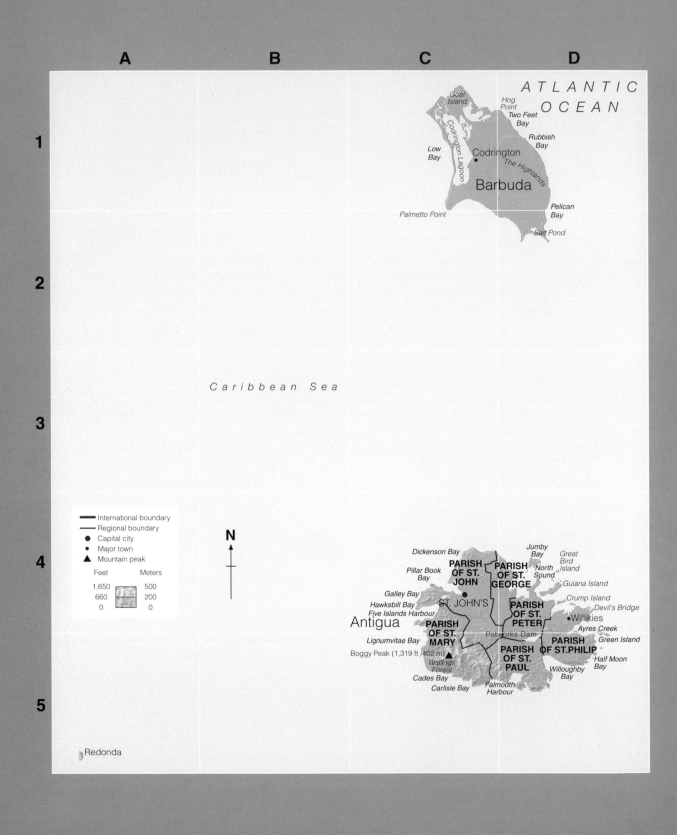

A   B   C   D

1

Goat Island

Codrington Lagoon

Hog Point
Two Feet Bay

A T L A N T I C
O C E A N

Rubbish Bay

Low Bay

Codrington

The Highlands

Barbuda

Palmetto Point

Pelican Bay

Salt Pond

2

C a r i b b e a n   S e a

3

International boundary
Regional boundary
● Capital city
• Major town
▲ Mountain peak

Feet   Meters
1,650   500
660   200
0   0

N

4

Dickenson Bay

PARISH OF ST. JOHN

PARISH OF ST. GEORGE

Jumby Bay

Great Bird Island

Pillar Book Bay

North Sound

Galley Bay

Guiana Island

ST. JOHN'S

PARISH OF ST. PETER

Crump Island

Hawksbill Bay

Devil's Bridge

Five Islands Harbour

•Willikies

Antigua

PARISH OF ST. MARY

Ayres Creek

Potworks Dam

Green Island

Lignumvitae Bay

PARISH OF ST.PHILIP

Boggy Peak (1,319 ft /402 m)▲

PARISH OF ST. PAUL

Half Moon Bay

Wallings Forest

Willoughby Bay

Cades Bay

Falmouth Harbour

Carlisle Bay

5

◗Redonda

MAP OF ANTIGUA AND BARBUDA

ECONOMIC ANTIGUA & BARBUDA

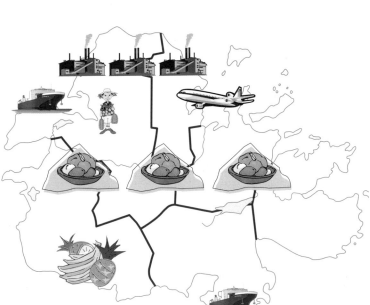

Industry

Crayfish

Dockyard

Factory

Sand

Agriculture

Pineapple &
Bananas

Pumpkin &
Sweet potatoes

Services

Airport

Tourism

ABOUT
THE ECONOMY

OVERVIEW
Tourism continues to be the driving force in the economy, earning over half of the country's total gross domestic product. Agricultural production and manufacturing contribute to the overall economy. However, economic growth depends heavily on developed nations, particularly the United States, which contributes to over one-third of all tourist arrivals.

GROSS DOMESTIC PRODUCT (GDP)
$857 million (2005 estimate)

GDP SECTORS
Services 74.3 percent, agriculture 3.8 percent, industry 22 percent (2002 estimate)

LAND AREA
171 square miles (443 square km)

AGRICULTURAL PRODUCTS
Cotton, bananas, coconuts, cucumbers, mangoes, sugarcane, pumpkin, sweet potatoes

CURRENCY
1 Eastern Caribbean dollar (EC) = 100 cents
Notes: 5, 10, 20, 50, 100 dollars
Coins: 1, 2, 5, 10, 25 cents; 1 dollar
USD 1 = 2.70 EC (October 2006)

INDUSTRIAL PRODUCTS
Textiles, rum, refined petroleum, paints, clothing, furniture, electrical components, alcohol, household appliances

LABORFORCE
30,000

UNEMPLOYMENT RATE
11 to 13 percent (2002 estimate)

INFLATION RATE
0.9 percent (2005 estimate)

EXTERNAL DEBT
$241 million (1999 estimate)

MAIN EXPORTS
Chemicals, machinery, transportation equipment, food, live animals, iron, steel

MAIN IMPORTS
Vegetables, fruit, meat, beverages, oil, machinery, chemicals, transportation equipment

TRADE PARTNERS
France, Germany, United States, Barbados, Canada, Singapore, Venezuela, Dominica, Japan, South Korea, Virgin Islands, United Kingdom, Poland, Jamaica

INTERNATIONAL AIRPORT
V. C. Bird International airport (Saint John's)

PORTS AND HARBORS
Deepwater Harbor, English Harbor, Jolly Harbor, Falmouth Harbor, Port Harbor

CULTURAL ANTIGUA & BARBUDA

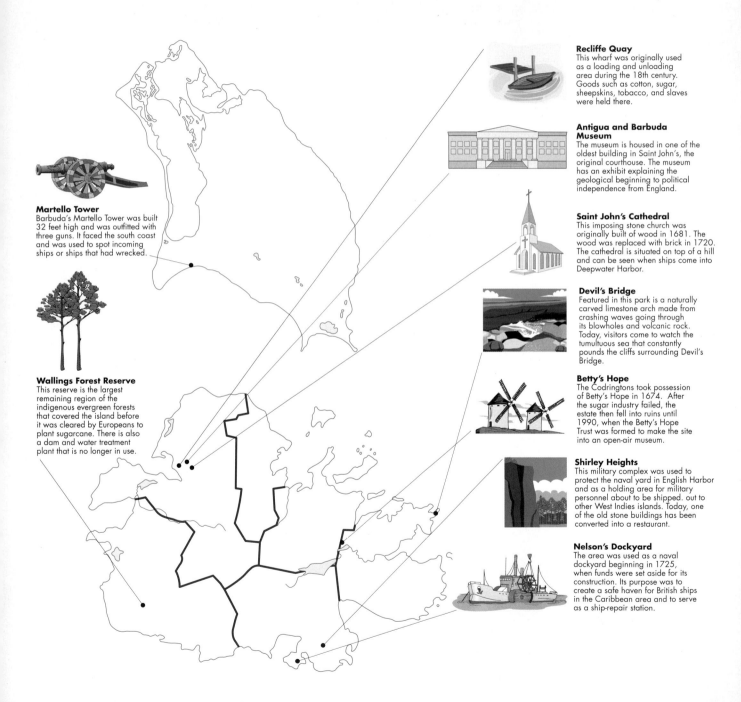

Recliffe Quay
This wharf was originally used as a loading and unloading area during the 18th century. Goods such as cotton, sugar, sheepskins, tobacco, and slaves were held there.

Antigua and Barbuda Museum
The museum is housed in one of the oldest building in Saint John's, the original courthouse. The museum has an exhibit explaining the geological beginning to political independence from England.

Saint John's Cathedral
This imposing stone church was originally built of wood in 1681. The wood was replaced with brick in 1720. The cathedral is situated on top of a hill and can be seen when ships come into Deepwater Harbor.

Devil's Bridge
Featured in this park is a naturally carved limestone arch made from crashing waves going through its blowholes and volcanic rock. Today, visitors come to watch the tumultuous sea that constantly pounds the cliffs surrounding Devil's Bridge.

Betty's Hope
The Codringtons took possession of Betty's Hope in 1674. After the sugar industry failed, the estate then fell into ruins until 1990, when the Betty's Hope Trust was formed to make the site into an open-air museum.

Shirley Heights
This military complex was used to protect the naval yard in English Harbor and as a holding area for military personnel about to be shipped. out to other West Indies islands. Today, one of the old stone buildings has been converted into a restaurant.

Nelson's Dockyard
The area was used as a naval dockyard beginning in 1725, when funds were set aside for its construction. Its purpose was to create a safe haven for British ships in the Caribbean area and to serve as a ship-repair station.

Martello Tower
Barbuda's Martello Tower was built 32 feet high and was outfitted with three guns. It faced the south coast and was used to spot incoming ships or ships that had wrecked.

Wallings Forest Reserve
This reserve is the largest remaining region of the indigenous evergreen forests that covered the island before it was cleared by Europeans to plant sugarcane. There is also a dam and water treatment plant that is no longer in use.

ABOUT
THE CULTURE

OFFICAL NAME
Antigua and Barbuda

CAPITAL
Saint John's

OTHER IMPORTANT CITIES
Codrington

PARISHES
Saint George, Saint John, Saint Mary, Saint Paul, Saint Peter, Saint Philip, and two dependencies: Barbuda and Redonda

POPULATION
About 69,108 (July 2006 estimate)

BIRTH RATE
16.93/1000 (2006 estimate)

LIFE EXPECTANCY
72.16 (2006 estimate)

ETHNIC GROUPS
The majority of population is of black African descent. The remainder is British, Portuguese, Lebanese, and Syrian.

RELIGIOUS GROUPS
Christian (the majority is Anglican, in addition to Protestant and Roman Catholic), Rastafarian, Buddhism, Baha'i Faith, Islam

PUBLIC HOLIDAYS
Independence Day (November 1), Labor Day (May 1), Vere Cornwall Bird Sr. Day (July 3), Carnival (end of July to beginning of August), Queen's Official Birthday (June 10)

POLITICAL PARTIES AND LEADERS
Antigua Labor Party or ALP (Vere Cornwall Bird Sr., founder and priminister, 1981 93; Lester Bryant Bird, prime minister, 1994-2004); Barbudans for a Better Barbuda (Ordrick Samuel); Barbuda People's Movement or BPM (Thomas H. Frank), Barbuda People's Movement for Change (Arthur Nibbs); United Progressive Party or UPP (Baldwin Spencer) which is a coalition of three parties— Antigua Caribbean Liberation Movement or ACLM, Progressive Labor Movement or PLM, United National Democratic Party or UNDP.

ADMINISTRATIVE DIVISIONS
Parishes: Saint George, Saint John, Saint Mary, Saint Paul, Saint Peter, Saint Philip Dependencies: Barbuda, Redonda

LANGUAGES
English (official), Antiguan Creole (patois), other dialects

NATIONAL FLOWER
Agave lily

TIME LINE

IN ANTIGUA AND BARBUDA	IN THE WORLD

1875 B.C.
Stone Age, people populate Barbuda.

775 B.C.
Ceramic Age starts slowly in Antigua. Peaceful farmers originating from Venezuela known as the Arawak begin to arrive.

753 B.C.
Rome is founded.

1000
The Chinese perfect gun powder and begin to use it in warfare.

1200
A new group of Amerindians arrive called the Caribs. They begin mixing with the existing Arawaks.

1493
Antigua is claimed by Spain by Columbus and named Santa Maria la Antigua.

1530
Beginning of transatlantic slave trade organized by the Portuguese in Africa.

1558–1603
Reign of Elizabeth I of England

1620
Pilgrims sail the *Mayflower* to America.

1632
Antigua becomes an English colony led by Sir Thomas Warner.

1674
Sir Christopher Codrington arrives from Barbados and establishes a large sugar plantation on Antigua.

1678
Barbuda becomes an English colony.

1685
Christopher and John Codrington are allowed to lease the island of Barbuda from King Charles II.

1689-98
Christopher Codrington serves as the governor of Antigua.

1705
The Codringtons are granted a renewed lease for Barbuda by Queen Anne for 99 years.

1776
U.S. Declaration of Independence

IN ANTIGUA AND BARBUDA	IN THE WORLD
1785-92 The majority of buildings seen today in English Harbor are built.	**1789–99** The French Revolution
1834 Slavery in Antigua and Barbuda is abolished.	**1861** The U.S. Civil War begins.
1870 Barbuda is united with Antigua.	**1914** World War I begins.
1939 The Antigua Trades and Labor Union is founded.	**1939** World War II begins.
1943 Vere Cornwall Bird is elected as the president of the Antigua Trades and Labor Union.	**1945** The United States drops atomic bombs on Hiroshima and Nagasaki.
1958-62 Antigua becomes part of the Federation of the West Indies.	**1949** The North Atlantic Treaty Organization (NATO) is formed.
1981 Independence by Antigua and Barbuda is achieved, and Vere Cornwall Bird is named the first Prime Minister.	**1991** Breakup of the Soviet Union **1997** Hong Kong is returned to China. **2001** Terrorists crash planes in New York, Washington, D.C., and Pennsylvania.
2002 Lester Bird has a dispute with leaders of the UPP. He initiates a libel suits that he later drops. An ALP member of Parliament demands that Lester Bird resign as prime minister.	**2003** War in Iraq begins.
2004 General elections are held, and Baldwin Spencer of the UPP is sworn in as prime minister.	
2005 Ground is broken for the construction of the Vivian Richards Stadium, which is due for completion in 2007 for the Cricket World Cup.	

GLOSSARY

bakkra
A white plantation owner.

bicameral
Having two legislative groups of lawmakers.

cassava
An edible, starchy root.

coral reefs
Limestone structures made of coral animals.

desalination
The process of purifying salt or brackish water by removing the dissolved salts.

emancipation
To be freed from another's control.

erosion
The wearing away of land or soil by the action of wind, water, or ice.

hybrid
A mix of something.

linguists
Specialists in the science of languages.

litany
A telling of facts and details.

money-laundering
Disguising money earned from criminal activities.

mollusk
An animal that has a soft body and no backbone that is often enclosed in a hard shell.

mulattoes
A term used to designate people of mixed black and white parentage.

offshore banking
This type of banking allows a person or a corporation to set up a bank account and keep the information of the contents and transactions of that account confidential.

regatta
A series of boat races.

satire
The use of sarcasm or humor to criticize or make fun of someone or something including ideas.

scrimshaw
Carving materials such shells, bones, or ivory.

slander
Speaking a falsehood of someone that harms their reputation.

statutory commission
A commission established by a legislative body.

survey
A detailed study by gathering and examining information.

FURTHER INFORMATION

BOOKS

Etherington, Melanie. *The Antigua and Barbuda Companion.* Brooklyn, NY: Interlink Books, 2003.
Lawrence, Joy. *The Way we Talk and other Antiguan Folkways.* Rev. ed. Antigua: J. Lawrence, 2003.

WEB SITES

Antigua and Barbuda. http://www.countrystudies.us/caribbean-islands/92.htm
Barbudaful. http://www.barbudaful.net
Facts about Antigua and Barbuda. http://worldfacts.us/Antigua-Barbuda.htm
Government of Antigua and Barbuda. http://www.ab.gov.ag/gov_v2/
Museum of Antigua and Barbuda. http://www.antiguamuseums.org/
National symbols of Antigua and Barbuda. http://www.environmentdivision.info/department/national_symbols.htm
Portals to the World. http://www.loc.gov/rr/international/hispanic/antigua/antigua.html
The Daily Observer. http://www.antiguaobserver.com/

BIBLIOGRAPHY

Ali, Arif, ed. *Antigua and Barbuda: A Little Bit of Paradise*. London: Hansbib Publications, 1999.

Etherington, Melanie. *The Antigua and Barbuda Companion*. Brooklyn, NY: Intelink Books, 2003.

———. *Caribbean Creoles*. Antigua: Antigua Printing and Publishing, 2003.

Europa World Year Book, 2005. 46th ed. Vol. 1. New York: Routledge, 2005.

Lawrence, Joy. *The Way We Talk and Other Antiguan Folkways*. Antigua: Antigua Printing and Publishing, 2002.

Marx, Jennifer. *Pirates and Privateers of the Caribbean*. Malabar, FL: Krieger, 1992.

Nicholson, Desmond V. *Africans to Antiguans: The Slavery Experience*. Museum of Antigua and Barbuda, 2003.

Smith, Keithlyn B. and Fernando C. Smith. *To Shoot Hard Labour*. ON, Canada: Edan's Publishers, Scarborough, 1986.

Turner, Barry, ed. *Statesman's Yearbook 2006*. 142nd ed. New York: Palgrave Macmillan, 2005.

World Book Encyclopedia, 2005. Chicago: World Book, 2005.

World Factbook 2005. Washington, DC: Brassey's, 2005.

Worldmark Encyclopedia of Cultures and Daily Living, 1998. Detroit: Gale Research, 1998.

INDEX